# THE CURIOUS CASE OF THE CONSTIPATED CAT

## and other true stories of answered prayer.

by

Barrie Lawrence

**Grosvenor House**
**Publishing Limited**

The book cover picture is copyright to Derek Blois
Cover design by Derek Blois

This book is published by
Grosvenor House Publishing Ltd
28-30 High Street, Guildford, Surrey, GU1 3EL.
www.grosvenorhousepublishing.co.uk

A CIP record for this book
is available from the British Library

ISBN 978-1-78623-722-4

This book is dedicated, with deep gratitude, to the evangelist Don Double and his late wife Heather, my spiritual parents for decades, my friends for eternity.

Also by Barrie Lawrence

THERE MUST BE MORE
TO LIFE THAN THIS          New Wine (2012)

A DENTIST'S STORY          Grosvenor House (2014)

PATIENTS FROM HEAVEN –
and Other Places          Grosvenor House (2015)

# Contents

# Foreword

"It's a coincidence," said my atheist sort-of-relation. (What a complex world we live in these days). "It's psychosomatic," said a family member, of presumably liberal Christian persuasion. I suppose there were those who said very similar things two thousand years ago when Jesus walked this earth, performing miracles that met the needs of those who suffered from hunger, sickness, internal torment, broken relationships, bereavement and tax bills. But it starts to irritate, just a bit, when people keep saying it. My response to them tends to be, "Coincidence after coincidence? Stop kidding yourself. Come on, get real, and get involved with this wonderful mighty God who answers prayer."

It was three years ago that my first book was published. It was largely testimony, and had so many good reviews... mainly! There was just one professing Christian who reviewed it on amazon with more than a suggestion of sarcasm. Would I ever dare write again? Could I?

I used to give after-dinner talks to entertain – to make people laugh, and occasionally shock them. I also gave evangelistic talks, and preached, usually giving an appeal for salvation, healing, etc. at the conclusion. In fact, one church was quite specific with its request "We would like 60% funny, 40% spiritual, and no appeal at the end please." What an evening it was with around 150 people, about half of them unbelievers, crammed into a very rural Norfolk (UK) pub restaurant, laughing at some of my stories, listening attentively to the testimony, challenges and gospel, and then engaging in conversation with the Christians who had invited them.

I gathered my stories. Some were funny, others cute, or concerned patients who I considered remarkable. Some were simply disgusting, and usually involved false teeth. I put them together and found my second book taking shape. It was an autobiography, darting from catching mice with my bare hands, to drilling teeth, to converting from atheist to Christian, to people losing their false teeth down the toilet. People called it fun, and I was on the radio and television. Well, locally. And the third book was thumbnail sketches of patients who, in my opinion, were admirable, weird, exemplary, crazy, virtuous, or, rarely, nasty. But it was written from a Christian perspective. It had to be, because Jesus had radically changed my life, by changing me, in October 1965.

"It's a coincidence," and "It's psychosomatic," were silly responses to unequivocal answers to prayer. Many of my friends just said, "Praise God," but there were those others. So I started noting down when prayer was answered, and then I thought back to other occasions when the God we read about in the Bible had answered my cries for help. I added a few of the more remarkable incidents that close, reliable friends told me about. Some were overwhelming, but others rather underwhelming. That's because I am a normal, ordinary person living a normal, ordinary life. There have been financial challenges, sickness and divorce, but also a sick much-loved pussycat, and a visitor who had to work too many hours. Big needs and mundane needs – all are important to us and therefore all are important to our loving Father in heaven. And somehow, these incidents of clearly answered prayer have grown into a book. I hope that the sceptical will pause and give more serious thought to these happenings, and that Christians will be encouraged to really step out in prayer, and in doing so be wonderfully surprised by our mighty God.

Come on, get real, and see just what our God can do! He is mighty. He is all-powerful. His Name is Jesus, and he will amaze you!

# People and Names

When I consider the things that the Lord has done in my life – my quality of life compared with that prior to knowing him, the sense of fulfilment, healing from IBS, restoration after letting him down, and more than a thousand other blessings – I want to shout it out and tell the world. So do most others I know – but not all. There are various reasons for this, from persecution and mocking (why did previous friends laughingly call me 'Vicar' when I said I had become a Christian?), disillusionment, clinical depression, and suchlike. But most want to shout it out! I do.

Quite a number of people walk across the pages of this book. Where it is helpful, I have used their real names, after asking their approval first. Others are people who walked into our lives, and then walked out again, *en passant*, so to speak. I have referred to such people as 'a man' or 'a woman' or 'a couple' or personalised them somewhat by using names such as Tom, Dick, Harriet and similar.

One man with a great story to tell, said, "Just write it down and publish it mate. Please do. You know my story and I trust you." It was a whole chapter, and I felt it best to send it to him for perusal anyway. The result? – a text from his wife telling me it was 'inappropriate'. So the book lost a chapter, and the kingdom lost an opportunity to proclaim what a wonderful God we have. Well, at least through the pages of this book.

But Malcolm also had a great story to tell, and he and his wife Moira sat down with me to ensure I really had 'got it right'. Listening to this quiet, modest couple speak, and reading through their story later, only enhances the sense of awe I feel at what God can do to make a difference in the lives of ordinary people; people like Malcolm, Moira, Wendy, me – and *you*.

All the stories in this book are true, and generally I have used people's real names. However, as outlined above, in some cases I have omitted them or substituted others. But nearly all the stories here come from my own experience, and the central character's name is JESUS!

# INTRODUCTION

## *Just Coincidences? – Come On!*

Malcolm was a builder, but also a pilot. In fact, he had a flying school. Some businessmen had asked him to fly them to meetings in various parts of the UK, and now he was with 5 of them in his plane on a runway at RAF Valley in North Wales, unable to take off because of dense fog. The control tower radioed him and told him to go back to the hotel as nothing and nobody would be taking off that day. "Sorry – we have to abandon this flight today," he explained to his passengers.

"But Jesus controls the weather, and gives us authority" piped up Colin from the back. "Let's take that authority now," and Colin told the fog to lift 'in Jesus Name!' Around 15 minutes later the fog lifted, the control tower announced they could take off, and a somewhat bemused Malcolm pulled back on the throttle, nosed up into a clear blue sky, and flew his passengers back to Norwich.

Back home, Malcolm telephoned the airport and thanked them for their help with his visit there. "You're the lucky one," they told him with a chuckle. "The fog unexpectedly lifted, and we gave you clearance to take off, which you did. But twenty minutes later the fog descended again for the rest of the day, just like the forecast said, and we are still closed now."

Colin prayed. The fog lifted. What a coincidence!

\* \* \*

"Come round for tea next Sunday, and we'll toast crumpets over the fire and drown them in butter!" It was Sid and Judy's first time at our church, and I wanted them to feel welcome.

They duly arrived, and we enjoyed tea, crumpets and good humour. But as the afternoon progressed, there were tears as the subject of their son came up. He was estranged, addicted, and on a slippery slope leading to the mortuary. We prayed together before they left.

The next Sunday when we arrived at church, we saw there was a rather smart young man standing with Sid and Judy. Guess who?

What a coincidence!

\* \* \*

Bathsheba had been my first real pet, and she had outlived the other two cats that had become part of our household after her. And now my beautiful Siamese was languishing on her rug, unable to eat or indeed, to pass anything, and the vet said that 'her insides were no longer working' and this was the end. She was 15, which I was told made her quite an elderly Siamese lady. Before leaving for the surgery that morning, I felt a sudden urge to reach out my hand towards her and pray that the power of God would come upon her and 'clean her out'.

When I returned home at lunchtime, I could hardly believe what I saw – and smelt! And Bathsheba was howling around my ankles, asking to be fed. Guess what had happened.

What a coincidence!

\* \* \*

Supper had been good – excellent food prepared by wonder-wife Wendy, and a buzz of conversation as we got to know Duane (not his real name), a somewhat Bohemian gentleman, and his more conventional partner. Now we were around the log fire in our sitting room and the atmosphere changed, as Cherie fought back tears and spoke of a rift in their family that was clearly causing great distress. I suggested we prayed, and knelt beside them by the sofa.

The next time we saw Duane and Cherie, they excitedly told us how the person concerned had texted them a reconciliatory message while they were with us. On returning home, they had found the text on Cherie's mobile phone, flashing away on a table and giving the time of the text – exactly the time we had prayed together for this.

What an amazing coincidence!

\* \* \*

Bob and Sue were new to our church and life was not easy for them. So they came to supper at our home, with wonder-wife Wendy serving up more excellent fayre while we got to know one another a little better.

Then on to the sitting room, log fire and coffee. "We'll have to go soon," said Bob. "I have to work tonight." We expressed surprise, as we understood he had worked all day.

"You're right," said Sue. "He has to work all hours, some unpaid, and he's tired out with it."

I suggested we pray, and Wendy and I drew our chairs alongside the sofa and proceeded to bring the situation to the Lord.

Less than three minutes later, the husband's phone rang. It was his work... and guess what they said? The situation there had changed, and they no longer required him to work that evening.

"That was quick," said Sue. It certainly was.

What an amazing coincidence!

\* \* \*

It was the early days of the Internet for me, and I found I could converse with people around the world, even in Australia, by typed messages in 'real time'. One of my new Christian friends, Greg, who lived in Australia, sent me a message, asking if I could pray for his marriage as after many years of tolerating each other, he and his wife had decided to separate and divorce. But he felt it was all so wrong.

I emailed that I would do so, turned my chair away from the computer and prayed to the God of the Bible. As I did so, the email arrived nine and a half thousand miles away in Australia. At that moment, Greg's wife walked into his study, caressed his shoulders and ... guess what she said?

What a coincidence!

\* \* \*

We live in a world that is heavily influenced by the media, and the prevailing fashion for scepticism about all things spiritual. We personally know one man in particular who is almost aggressive in his refutation of anything the Lord has done in my life or anybody else's – or, in fact, of anything the Lord has *ever* done. So, when I speak of how, following the laying on of hands and prayer, I was healed of an 'incurable' (the consultant's words) disease around twenty years ago, and have neither suffered pain nor taken any tablets since, he explains that it is just a coincidence. Likewise, Wendy and I have told him how, following a complex fracture, a boy's arm was fixed with plates and metal pins, leaving it immoveable and painful. Yet the arm simply straightened out in front of us when we prayed for it, and again our friend explains that it is just a coincidence. And with regard to the other instances related above, he explains that they are coincidences. So likewise with innumerable other answers to prayer, healings, miracles and strong indications of the presence and power of the God we read of in the Bible, he explains that they are merely coincidences.

\* \* \*

We used to live in an age where the default position of most people in the UK was Christian. However, I write in the second decade of the twenty-first century, at which time a most significant change has taken place in the worldview held by so many people here, not least the media. The result is that the default position of most people today is secular. If prayer is answered, if miracles happen, if God intervenes in people's lives... it is simply a coincidence.

I will not try to argue a case for the God of the Bible as he is well able to make himself known to those whose hearts and minds are open. To me, the evidence is quite overwhelming. But for people who believe in remarkable coincidences, I would like to entertain them with a selection from my own experience.

And of course, there are also those of us who will be tempted to explain the coincidence with... wow, it's a miracle!

(I have used the term 'the God of the Bible'. Why? – because I have found the term 'God' to be rather ambiguous. "I believe in God," some say, and then proceed to speak of him as a divine but impotent being who cannot intervene supernaturally today, or perhaps imply he is a divine, benign Softie, who would never get angry, let alone preside over judgement as described in scripture. So I sometimes clarify, with the term, 'the God of the Bible' – he loves us, he can be provoked to anger, he is as described in the Bible – and can do absolutely *ANYTHING!*)

\* \* \*

William Temple was an archbishop in the Church of England, and he made a quote, which became well-known amongst Bible believing Christians in the mid-nineteenth century. He said, "When I pray, coincidences happen. When I don't pray, coincidences don't happen." I heartily agree with what he said, and for the past year or two, as I have mentioned already, have jotted down occasions when I have prayed and 'coincidences' have happened. I have also thought back to previous times when I have prayed, and 'coincidences' have happened. And friends of mine have had this experience too – over and over again. But of course, they are not coincidences at all; they are simply Almighty God listening to his children, and doing what a good Father does – answering them.

Some of these examples are quite mundane everyday matters, such as driving by mistake on the wrong side of the road. That proved rather dangerous, but wait until you read what happened. Other answers were quite dramatic, such as a deformed arm being healed.

Wendy and I are, with all due respect to Wendy, two very ordinary people. We went to State schools, one of us passed the eleven plus exam (just, at the second attempt) and the other didn't. We both worked at nine to five jobs, except that one of us was also on shift work involving nights quite often. One of us earned quite a lot of money at times, but we have both known the feeling of uncertainty that comes with greatly reduced finances. We had both been happily married before going through the heartbreak and trauma of divorce. We met in later life, and cannot believe the contentment and fulfillment we have known since marrying around twelve years ago (at the time of writing). The main reason for our joy and fulfillment is that our lives were radically changed when we gave ourselves to the living God, who changes lives, heals sicknesses, meets needs and – answers prayers. As husband and wife, we see ourselves as a team, and function within the kingdom of God as such.

Romance? Oh yes, we are more than normal in that department, having honeymooned on safari in Africa, and enjoying most of our evening meals at home by candlelight. But we have scores and scores of people passing through our home, often for meals as well as for times of worship and prayer, and we travel to churches and meetings, not always in the UK, where, in addition to enjoying getting to know lots of lovely people, we also pray for those with needs.

Sometimes we do not receive an answer at the time, and sometimes we do.

So here are a selection of 'coincidences' – answers to prayer and other acts of God where there has been healing, provision, direction and suchlike, the mundane and the amazing, the underwhelming and the overwhelming, the everyday and the occasional 'special'. Be encouraged to step out and pray for people and situations if, like us, you are an ordinary person. We read in scripture that God does not call many wealthy, sophisticated, or worldly-wise people. He specialises in people like you and me, and he specialises in miracles. So I have written a few chapters in section two of things that we have found helpful – well, *essential* really – in getting heard in heaven and seeing answers on earth.

May the Lord bless you richly in your walk with him, and may you too experience the miracles God grants in response to the prayers of his children.

# PART ONE

Coincidences? Psychosomatic healings? Part One is a series of incidents that we have experienced, and a few from some of our friends, involving two frozen shoulders, two people with broken arms, a terminally sick pussycat, broken relationships, work overload, a cancelled take-off due to fog, irritable bowel, Crohn's Disease, financial needs and challenges, wanting a husband, wanting a wife, not wanting divorce... and a whole lot more. Following prayer, there was a dramatic change in each situation, because Jesus still works miracles today.

Read on, and be amazed at what God can do. And remember – what he does for others, he can do for you!

# Chapter 1

## Signs in the Sitting Room

I have been left with a sense of awe at what the Lord has been doing in our sitting room. *Liberty!*, the church that meets in our home, has been going for around three and a half years at the time of writing. Wayne, a rugby coach, asked for prayer for his foot, which was painful and intermittently numb. We got down on the floor, laid hands on it and prayed. The next day I phoned him and he told me it was better. I asked if he had injured it that weekend, and he replied, "No. About 18 months ago". Wow – I thought he had injured it that weekend, but he had in fact been suffering with it for a year and a half. And after the laying on of hands and prayer to God, it immediately cleared up. What a God!

A lady in the meeting had pain in her neck and shoulders such that if I laid my hand on her to pray for her, she would shout and move away. An evangelist called Ash Kotecha was visiting, and prayed for this lady. The power of God impacted her and she crashed to the floor. I thought how dreadful this was – surely she would be in agony forever now! But no, the Lord simply healed her, and she has had no more trouble from her shoulder or neck since. That was two and a half years ago now. Just a coincidence?

At the same meeting Ash prayed for a man with bladder problems. Some time later he told us he had been healed and was still healed. Another amazing coincidence.

\* \* \*

I also think about the way so many people have said that they feel his presence and closeness here. A rather troubled lady came round to see us about eighteen months ago, and I enquired if I could just lay my hand on her and ask the Lord to touch her. As I did so, she started laughing, and continued for around 25 minutes. The Lord did her good, and she said she must come round for a cup of tea again as she now felt wonderful!

On three occasions people have told me they have seen one or more angels in our sitting room; on several occasions when there have been a dozen of us praising, people have felt there were several times that number; once a lady detected a powerful and beautiful fragrance in the room, and looked around to see who had opened a perfume bottle (but there was not, of course); and on another occasion, a breeze was felt though no-one was moving and there were no draughts. Any one or two of these phenomena might be seen as suspect, but with so many amongst a relatively small number of people, they cannot be so easily dismissed as 'coincidences' or 'imaginations'.

It was in our sitting room that we prayed with Duane and Cherie about the rift in their family (see *Introduction*), and at the precise time that we were praying, the estranged member of the family texted Cherie to ask to come round in order to effect a reconciliation. Can one go on forever calling answered prayer a coincidence? Some people do – but I think that is so sad!

Bob and Sue (also mentioned in the *Introduction*) were sitting on the same sofa in our sitting room when we prayed about his evening's work, and it was cancelled. Immediately. Some people might call it a coincidence, but I call it answered prayer. We have a God who is alive in heaven and active on earth. He hears people speaking to him, and he answers those requests. Not always as we expect, and not always immediately, though sometimes it is both of these.

\* \* \*

Pam, a lady from the USA asked if she could come and stay with us. She had read my first book, *THERE MUST BE MORE TO LIFE THAN THIS!* and felt that she would receive something special from the Lord if she came to stay. I pointed out that we each receive from the Lord through one another, and there was nothing extraordinary about us, except that like *all* God's children, we are special. She stayed with us nearly a week, and on the penultimate day of her stay, our church gathered after having asked the Lord for prophetic words for Pam. A number of these words were shared with her, and after we had prayed, Jim asked Pam specifically, "Have you been baptised in the Holy Spirit and spoken with tongues?" Pam had not, and so he laid his hand on her and prayed, and as he did so, Pam virtually exploded in praise to God in a whole new language. As a believer, Pam had the Holy Spirit dwelling within her before this event, but that afternoon God had impacted her, and she would never be quite the same again!

We have just (at the time of writing) received an email from Pam in which she excitedly speaks of the real revelation of grace that she has come into. How good the Lord is to undeserving people – amazingly, incredibly good. Pam's email was alive with the Spirit, and Wendy and I felt so excited reading it.

\* \* \*

And then there was Sid and Judy and their son Gary. (Not their real names). I enjoy meeting new people, as well as the continuing friendship of those I first met weeks, or more often, decades ago. My enjoyment of the former would find me lurking just inside the entrance doors of the church I was a part of for many years, and looking out for people I had not seen before, or who were relatively new to our gatherings. Sid and Judy walked in, and I was almost certain I had never seen them before. I pounced! "Good morning. Great to see you

5

here today. My name's Barrie. Have I met you before?" Their response was almost predictable, "No. It's our first time. We live just a few miles down the road, and thought we would see what this church is like," said Sid. In fact, they did not live far from me, and in a community that I wanted the church to reach into – at last we had a contact there. I explained that they lived near me, and said it would be good to get to know each other.

"Come round for tea next Sunday, and we'll toast crumpets over the fire and drown them in butter!" I said by way of invitation.

It was the following Sunday afternoon, and having consumed two to three fire-toasted, butter-drenched crumpets apiece, we settled back in our chairs, drinking tea and getting to know one another. The usual preliminaries included questions about family, and it was soon clear that Judy was in some degree of distress.

After the break-up of his marriage, their son Gary had hit the bottle before progressing to even more serious addictions. He lived some distance away, was estranged from his parents, and appeared to be on the slippery slope to the mortuary. I suggested that the four of us pray about the situation, and there and then we asked the Lord for peace and strength for the parents, and a complete change of heart for the son. Gary had once been an active member of an evangelical church.

My wife and I were away the following weekend, but were back in church the Sunday after that. We looked for our new friends Sid and Judy, and spotted them sitting towards the front. But between them sat a rather smart young man, well-dressed and well-groomed.

"Meet our son Gary," said Sid. "He's come home to live with us. He came here last week, but you were away." "Really nice to meet you, Barrie," said Gary. And at the end of the meeting he came over and asked, "Could you pray for me please? Now? I really want to move on with God."

I saw Sid and Judy by themselves a little later, and they brought me up to date with what had happened. They had continued praying together for Gary after the afternoon of crumpets and prayer at our home. A few days later, they received a telephone call from their son who told them that he really wanted to get free of his addictions, and asked if he could move in with them. He arrived the following day, and as far as they knew had not touched alcohol, tobacco or drugs since. In fact, they were praying together again as a family.

It was not all plain sailing from that time, and Gary relapsed, then recommitted to Christ, then relapsed... At times the situation was dire, and once or twice his relationship with his parents hit an all time low. But at around twelve years on at the time of writing, Gary is in a stable relationship with a partner and growing family, and active in the life of a church in our local city.

Despite the relapses, Gary has really moved on from the grave position he was in when I first heard of him. The four of us prayed together to the God we read about in the Bible – and a few days later, their son's life turned around so dramatically and unexpectedly. How can sceptics and cynics seriously cast doubt upon the existence of our Heavenly Father? He is real. He answers prayer, especially the cries of his children. Come on – get real!

* * *

I have been a member of the FGB for over three decades. The FGB? – the Full Gospel Businessmen's Fellowship. We are an interdenominational fellowship of businessmen who have each had a life-changing experience of Jesus Christ. 'Full Gospel'? – we believe that there is much more to the gospel than being 'born again', and that we should expect miracles, signs and wonders from our unchanging God. Typically, we have a dinner once a month at which we 'tell our story'. So we have farmers, doctors, builders, gardeners, plumbers, mechanics, geologists, grocers, electricians, architects, teachers, clerical workers.... and we invite our friends to hear other businessmen tell their story. In some areas, the FGB might have breakfasts or luncheons, but there is usually food involved as well as 'telling our story'. Food – it has been suggested that this is the reason we are called the *full* gospel businessmen!

Our local FGB meets once a month at a local hotel for an evening dinner, and usually one week before the dinner, we have a meeting at our home. The meeting at our home? – food! But more than food, as the main focus of the evening is to pray for the following week's dinner. Wendy enthuses over cooking, and usually between fifteen and thirty-five people arrive for a choice of four hot main courses followed by puddings. It is called a 'fellowship evening' and there is certainly plenty of conversation and laughter round the table during the meal.

We then proceed to the sitting room, where we have a time of praise, worship and prayer. We ask the Lord to 'come down' and be with us – to make his presence known. I play the guitar (badly) and lead the singing (loudly) because I enjoy praising the Lord (wildly) for the good, gracious, merciful and at times amazing things he has done in my life. We love these times, and it often feels that the Spirit of God himself comes and joins in with us. I believe he does. After the praise and worship, we pray for the coming evangelistic dinner, and also seek to respond to anything the Lord says to us during our time, by way of prophetic word, or tongue and interpretation, or word of knowledge or similar.

Around two years ago, at the time of writing, the meeting was almost over and relatively quiet, when a mobile phone gave a little bleep. Malcolm stood up and asked us if we could pray, as the text message he had received was to inform him that his brother had just been diagnosed with a brain tumour, and had a poor prognosis. We turned to prayer, bringing Malcolm's brother to the Lord.

\* \* \*

It was some time after this that a man called David started coming to our meetings. Not every meeting, but occasionally. At the end of one such meeting, he approached me holding his mobile phone in his hand. He asked if he could have a word, and told me that he had just received a text. The father of a friend of his had been suffering from depression, and he had just received the diagnosis. He had a brain tumour. David asked if we could pray.

I had completely forgotten the incident of a year previously, and David knew nothing about it. I called for silence, and asked people to join us in prayer, explaining about David's text. Immediately Malcolm stood up and reminded us of the almost identical circumstances a year before. His brother was not expected to be alive by this time, but was getting stronger and doing well, which gave us great faith for the man we heard about that Friday night. A coincidence? The chances of receiving two almost identical text messages a year apart, to different people, in the same room, during the same meeting...... one in a million... trillion? Why can people not see God in this?

Malcolm's brother improved in health sufficiently to return to a reasonably normal life-style, and whilst attending one of our FGB dinners, gave his life to Jesus. It was a year or so after this that he went downhill in health, and passed on into the presence of the Lord he had come to love. I have not seen David for some time in order to catch up with news of his friend's father.

\* \* \*

A friend called John was having serious problems urinating, which was a complication arising from another medical problem. Unable to get to our monthly FGB prayer meeting, he telephoned and asked for prayer. We shared this need with the group that gathered, and at 7.30 p.m. entered a time of praise and worship, then moving into prayer, and bringing our much loved John to the Lord.

The next day I received the following email –

*Dear Barrie and Wendy*

*If you prayed for me last night, your prayers were answered! The catheter came out in the morning (a nice lapsed Seventh Day Adventist District nurse). She is now re-programmed! But no real improvement in waterworks and great pain until about 8pm when the waters of the deep opened up at last! It is great to be nearly back to normal!*

*Many thanks!*

*John*

But it was not Barrie and Wendy – it was Jesus!

\* \* \*

A centurion told Jesus that he was not worthy to have him under his roof (Matthew 8:8), and I feel the same. Yet he has brought healings, joy, laughter, visions, hope, encouragement.... and so much more into the lives of those who gather here. Loads and loads of coincidences? – I think not.

The God of the Bible is unchanging. If you never have before, turn to him today and surrender your life to serving him. You'll never be the same again, and you'll never regret it.

# Chapter 2

# *That Same Song*

Simon had been an elder in a church for many years, and was starting to feel that the Lord might be calling him elsewhere. And one day he heard a song – twice!

\* \* \*

Roy Lamark had arrived in the city years ago, when I was still in my thirties, married with a young family. In fact, Roy too was in his thirties with a young family, when he felt a call from heaven to come to Norwich to preach the gospel and gather those who came to Christ. The work prospered, and though there was not exponential growth, upwards of fifty people were meeting after a few years. Time passed, and Roy died at a fairly young age, after which a new pastor headed up the work. Then the pastor moved abroad and the church was led by half a dozen elders who met together just once a year. Simon was one of them, and he was becoming restless.

\* \* \*

Our own little church, called *Liberty!*, was having an outreach meeting in a church building in the next village. I was rather apprehensive, wondering whether people would actually come. Wendy and I had been part of a larger church in a town around seven miles from our home, until one night I had a vivid dream that Wendy and I felt was from the Lord, and that would mean us leaving our home church. But we are not 'short term' people, moving from church to church every few years, and we dragged our heels when it came to leaving. In fact, we stayed a further three years, and only when the leadership said that we were to sell our home and move to another town, did we seriously ask the Lord what *he* wanted us to do. He was silent, as he had already spoken – and his silence spoke volumes. So after twenty-five years in the same church, we said our Goodbyes and stayed at home. At home? Yes, Wendy and I stayed at home and worshipped, sang, prayed, broke bread (had 'communion'), and read the Bible together. We told people from our previous church not to follow us, as God was now doing a new thing. But others trekked out to where we lived on the outskirts of a tiny village in rural Norfolk, and during our first three years, around two hundred people passed through our sitting room. Many were drifters who tried every new church that came along, and others were addicts, depressives, people with broken relationships, and those marginalised by more conventional churches. There was also a core of people who felt the Lord call them to join us, and who therefore stayed.

I was at the outreach meeting, and relieved to see around thirty to forty people come in through the little porch. At the back was a tall man who looked round at the other people as though he felt out of place. I wondered whether he was a Christian, or maybe someone who was simply curious about whether God was real or not.

I welcomed the people, prayed and started strumming my guitar in a rousing song of praise to the Lord. Immediately the tall man threw his arms into the air, and beaming towards heaven, started singing. Yes – that man knew the Lord!

At the end of the meeting we chatted briefly. His name was Simon, he was an elder in a church in the city, but he wanted more fellowship. Could he come to one of our regular church meetings? Where did we meet? Where was our home?

So Simon decided that he would come and join us for one of our evening meetings, and asked the Lord to confirm that this was his will for him. He chose a convenient Sunday, and thought it wise to drive out in the morning to make sure he knew where we were. A house on the edge of a small village in rural Norfolk can be difficult to locate!

He drove a few miles out of the city and found our village. He turned into the lane that led to our home, and as he did so started singing a song – 'Come bless the Lord, all you servants of the Lord.' "Strange," he thought to himself. "I haven't sung that song for years and years. Why am I singing it now?" And he drove along the lane, noted where our home was, and returned to the city, still singing the same song.

That evening, Simon again drove out to our village, came into our sitting room and sat down with the other fifteen or so people who had gathered. I picked up my guitar, and started playing. The song? 'Come bless the Lord, all you servants of the Lord.'

After the meeting, Simon came over to me and almost immediately asked me why I had started with that song.

"I'm not sure really," I said. "I used to sing it around thirty years ago, and just these past few days it's been going around in my head. So I worked out the chords, and started out with it this evening."

Simon stared at me for a short while, and then told me of how he had sung it while driving past that morning. He had sung it for the first time in years, and had no idea why. Now he knew – and so did I! The Lord was showing Simon that he was in the right place at the right time, and I realised that too.

And though it was only for a season, I learnt a lot from Simon being with us, and he learnt a lot too, from what the Lord was doing amongst us at that time.

After around thirty years, we had both started singing the same song. One might even say that the Lord had shown us that we were both singing from the same song sheet. *His* song sheet.

Or you might just say – what a coincidence. But that would be rather silly, wouldn't it!

# Chapter 3

## *A Romance Restored.*

It was towards the end of the 1990s when I first got hooked up. I had been using a computer since 1983, when a Sinclair Spectrum had enabled me to play Space Invaders, and games where spiders chased me round the screen. Not a good idea for a man who suffered from arachnophobia anyway!

Then came a free offer that looked too good to refuse. A free computer. No catches or trickery – a free computer was offered to dentists in the UK by a company called Baker Heath. I thought about it quickly, and applied immediately. Surely there would be a stampede for the machines, and I wanted to be at the head of the queue. My computer duly arrived – but it did not do anything. I needed software. "What's software?" I enquired. "About £1,000," should have been their answer, and I duly forked out. And a little more to connect to the NHS dental HQ in order to speed up payments from them. And before I knew it, the software was out of date and needed replacing. "What for?" I enquired. "About £500," should have been their reply. Baker Heath! I always referred to them as Heath Robinson, but I was learning fast about the real cost of computing.

Can you remember the first time you played Solitaire ('Patience' in English) on your computer? And can you remember the first time you won? Of course you can, and so can I, watching with amazement as the cards tumbled across the screen in scintillating and mesmerising patterns at around

1.30 a.m. It was the same relatively primitive computer that took me into the Internet – the Worldwide Web.

A patient of mine called Peter was the first person I can recall speaking about it. He had co-authored a book on personal growth, and was now using the Internet to research for the courses he was running. He was amazed, astounded, totally gobsmacked (not a word dentists use very often) at what he found there. "You can read research papers in Sweden one minute, and be in Australia the next," he explained excitedly. "And you can send emails – they're like letters typed onto your screen – to the other side of the world in seconds. It's totally revolutionary."

And so it was that I too got hooked up. I did not understand it, but there were plenty of younger folk who did. In fact, the younger they were, the more they understood. Any person out of their teens was really too old and too past it. It was suggested that the average age of a computer operator in the UK was ten, and that that was also the optimum age for knowledge and helpfulness when one needed to learn more or have one's machine 'fixed'.

Like most of my peers, I explored what was 'out there'. I discovered that one could use emails like conventional letters, which were now referred to as 'snail mail', because they took so long to arrive compared with electronic mail flying around the globe at something approaching the speed of light. So I was told. And then there were 'messengers', where one could chat in 'real time' – it was like a telephone conversation, except we used typed words in place of spoken words. I also heard about chat-rooms, but steered clear as they were getting a bad press, so it seemed to me. I joined groups. With two Siamese cats that were like family, I was soon exchanging cat stories with others who shared my penchant for the creatures. But my greatest passion in life is for Jesus. It has been since October 1965, when I first came to faith in him, found he was real, and experienced my whole life being turned right way up. And so I found other Christians of all persuasions, from out and out fundamentalists, to liberal and social and political. I joined groups. I chatted. And just a few became 'almost friends'.

Greg was an interesting guy. He lived in Australia, lectured in agriculture at University, and had a smallholding. He was married to Rachel, and they had a teenaged daughter, Mandy. He explained that he did not share my evangelical faith – he was more of a liberal, but he loved God and wanted to live for him. We emailed from time to time, and occasionally messaged.

It was early in the year 2,000 when he emailed me, with a somewhat more serious tone to his words. Did I really believe that prayer 'worked'? Did God really hear us when we prayed to him? We corresponded, electronically, on the subject a time or two.

And then, one evening, I received an email from Greg, in which he opened his heart. He and Rachel had fallen in love over two decades earlier, and had married. Mandy had been born, and Rachel had spent more time with her and around the house as Greg had developed his career at the University. And the University was not exactly on the doorstep. Instead of absence causing the heart to grow fonder, it had the opposite effect, and as a result he and Rachel had grown apart and decided to divorce. Their relationship was cold. The tenderness had long gone. They would not divorce immediately, but in a couple of years or so when Mandy herself left home and went to University.

Yet it all seemed so wrong to Greg. Surely they should not only stand by their marriage vows, but also be seeking to find again the love they had once enjoyed together. So he asked me if I would seriously pray, asking the Lord to save his marriage. The request arrived in an email, and I had developed a routine in handling email requests for prayer. As it was so easy to say that I'd pray, and then forget, I usually wrote an email back, explaining that I would pray for the request as soon as I had hit the *SEND* key on the keyboard. I wrote this explanation to

Greg, hit *SEND* and turned away from the screen, praying and lifting my brother Greg and his marriage to the God who is with us, hears us, and answers. I then turned the computer off and went to bed.

\* \* \*

The next morning I checked my incoming emails before driving the seven and a half miles to my surgery for the day's work. Greg's name was amongst those that had arrived. I opened the email, and could hardly believe what I read.

Greg had been sitting at his computer, having sent me his prayer request. He felt very unsettled within at the prospect of divorce and all that it entailed. It was morning, and he was not expecting me to reply so soon, when *Ping*! An email had arrived, and it was from me. He opened it and started reading. I thanked him for his email. I thanked him for his prayer request. I would pray after hitting *SEND*. Then surely, he thought, I must be praying at that very time; 9,500 miles away, but praying to the God who was with each of us anyway.

He heard someone enter the room, and from the reflection in his monitor realised that it was Rachel. He remained facing the screen, and was surprised that she came right over to where he sat. She placed her hands on his shoulders, caressed them gently, and asked if they could sit together and talk. Surely, they should never have come to the place where they spoke of divorce. Was there no way back? Couldn't they rediscover the romance they had once enjoyed?

Greg felt overwhelmed with joy that his marriage could be saved, and that romance might actually be restored. They were going to talk more. And as for prayer being answered, this was way beyond his wildest expectations.

And mine!

\* \* \*

I could hardly contain my joy. Coincidence? Come on – if ever there was evidence of a God in heaven who was active on earth, and who heard the cry of his children and answered them with miracles... But some would say it was just a coincidence!

\* \* \*

We continued to email from time to time, and it seemed as if everything was going better than either of us had expected. And then with changing circumstances and other priorities, we lost touch.

\* \* \*

It was towards the end of 2012, and my first book was about to be published. A young man who I knew through church, had set up a website for me, and also a page on Facebook and links to Twitter. He encouraged me to write a regular blog. "What's a blog?" I asked, and he explained that it is a type of diary-made-public, where I would write on events in my life – and point people towards my book. It seemed like fun anyway, and I was soon tapping away.

Wendy and I were at that time enjoying a season of 'quick answers to prayer'. That is not the norm for us, but was for a purpose. Work was being carried out on our home, and the workmen were members of a cult. They were a captive audience, and the Lord gave me a lot to tell them. It was about that time that Duane and Cherie were reconciled with their family member, and Bob and Sue were blessed with a night when he did not have to work. I told the workmen all about it, and included these things in a blog.

But had I other examples of prayer that had been answered almost instantly? I thought of Greg and Rachel, and wrote out the amazing story. And then I stopped – what if they were no longer together? Maybe they had divorced in the end? Were they still alive, as over twelve years had passed? I felt I should try and find out what their situation was before publishing, but his email address had vanished along with the computer I had emailed him on when I had upgraded to a newer one. I knew nothing of transferring data in those days.

Just two days later an email arrived. Christmas was approaching and Greg had decided to catch up with old friends by sending out a newsletter. He and Rachel were enjoying running the smallholding, with less time now at University. Mandy was using her University degree to develop her own career. He and Rachel were involved in the life of a local church. He and Rachel... "Rachel and I..."

I emailed back with my own news, and enclosed a copy of the blog I had written, cataloging the events leading up to his reconciliation with Rachel – an almost immediate answer to prayer that was proffered 9,500 miles away. Yes, of course I could publish it. Yes, they were still together, and very much in love. Yes, what a wonderful God we have as Father.

* * *

I sat there almost dazed. I had a sense of awe at the God who had not only answered my prayer for the restoration of love and marriage for two cyber friends that I had never met, but also for the almost immediate update on their situation and permission to publish it.

No one can prove God to another person, but to me the evidence is overwhelming, and fills me with faith.

However, some people would say these happenings were just coincidences. Come on – get real!

# Chapter 4

## An Angel in Venice

Suddenly – he was there. He showed us the way. And suddenly – he was gone!

\* \* \*

Which is your favourite city? As a boy, Norwich, in the east of the UK was my favourite city. Well, it was my *only* city as I had not been anywhere else. We lived seven miles to the north of what is probably the only city in East Anglia, and if anyone had any doubt about the quality of the place, there were signs to inform us we were entering *Norwich, A Fine City*. And indeed it is, with its iconic Norman castle dominating the city since the eleventh century, the elegant Romanesque architecture of the cathedral, likewise dating from Norman times, and the quaint, cobbled streets lined with picturesque Tudor buildings. Also, of course, there are the Canaries, the city's football team. Later I trained in London, and stared with a sense of awe at Tower Bridge – it was just like I'd seen it on television.

Many years later, I had the opportunity to travel abroad, and coming from the backwaters of rural Norfolk, I felt rather like Marco Polo. I marvelled at the Parthenon atop the acropolis in Athens, and drooled at the Eastern romance of Istanbul astride the Bosphorus; I was mesmerised by the mysterious medinas of the ancient Moorish cities of north

Africa, alive with colour, fragrance and movement, and lived the dream in a whirlwind tour of Jerusalem, the city of God; from Prague to Peking, from Bangkok to Buenos Aires, from Moscow to Marrakech, every city had unique charm, beautiful architecture and style, and a history to match. But my favourite?

For many years Prague was my top city, with five very different, but enchanting quarters, each exuding a wealth of beauty and history, and all within walking distance of one another. Until I really discovered Venice. I had first visited there many years ago, and having somewhat modest finances at that time, stayed in Lido di Jesolo, some distance away from the city itself, traversing the Venetian lagoon on a water bus through dense clouds of mosquitos. A modest income? – I romanced the love of my life with a gondola ride through the stinking backwaters of the city, passing floating bottles and dead rats while the gondolier occasionally broke out into the Cornetto song, and we dined several blocks distant from the delights of St. Marks square.

Years later I met and married Wendy, who had never been to Venice. Wendy would tell people that we did not really have holidays – we had *adventures*. The Arctic, the Antarctic, deserts and jungles and rivers and mountains were the destinations that attracted and enthralled us. But we had to see Venice, and this time I could just about stretch to a hotel on the Grand Canal.

OK, it was a budget airline, but I did fork out for a limousine to meet us at the airport. There would be waterbuses servicing the canals once we arrived in the city itself, most Italians spoke English (didn't they?) and certainly the operators on the waterbuses spoke English (didn't they?), and we would be arriving in reasonable time during the evening.

We drove to Gatwick airport and checked in. On time, we were invited to board the plane. But we sat there, and sat there, and sat there. The pilot announced that there was a problem with the navigation equipment, but engineers had arrived to fix it. And we waited. The pilot announced that the problem was being fixed – and we waited. A little later, we were informed that a replacement navigation system was being fitted, and somewhat over two hours later, we took off.

Our limousine driver had followed the flight's progress, or lack of it, on his computer, and was waiting. We were whisked along the road that runs along the promontory from the airport to the city, and were informed that though few waterbuses were running at this time (well past midnight), we would not have to wait too long.

The waterbus duly arrived, and we told the 'conductor' the stop at which we needed to alight. But he did not speak English. Absolutely none! We gesticulated – and so did he! So we set off, and counted the stops we made until we estimated that we were at the one we needed. I produced euros, and shrugged my shoulders in a manner that said, "How much money do you want?" and the conductor shooed us away, obviously glad to see the back of the foreigners who could not speak his language.

So we stood at the waterbus stop, alone in the dark with the occasional lamp lighting up its little patch of territory and creating shadows for most others. And somewhere, somewhere within walking distance, with four cases, somewhere in the dark beyond, through gloomy passages, over little bridges and along narrow paths between towering buildings, was the hotel. But where?

We felt very vulnerable and very lonely standing by the canal and surveying the various possible routes open to us. And then, turning round to consider the options, there was a man. Just standing there. Going nowhere. Doing nothing.

We approached him, vaguely silhouetted in the Venetian night and unable to see his face in the dark.

"San Cassiano", I said, naming our hotel.

"Along that path, then turn left at the end. Soon, a right turn and keep looking on your left. There is a sign." The directions were given in a very comprehensible Italian accent

– but it *was* very comprehensible. (I am not sure precisely of the 'lefts' and 'rights', but you get the picture).

We started pulling our luggage along the path the man had directed, when I realised I had not thanked him. I turned round, but there was no-one there. The place where he had been standing was empty – and we had hardly started walking. Where had he gone? There was no-one in sight.

We thought no more of it, and following his directions, quickly found our hotel and felt greatly relieved.

What an excellent few days. A gondola ride along the more salubrious canals, tea in St. Mark's Square, a cruise around the lagoon, and a night at the opera enjoying La Traviata at a palazzo on the Grand Canal.

But who was the stranger? Suddenly – he was there. He showed us the way. And suddenly – he was gone.

Wendy and I believe it was an angel sent by God. Of course, some would call it a coincidence, that when we really needed help in a strange city in the middle of the night, there was a man who knew the way, and who spoke English, and was in the right place at the right time..... But they would, wouldn't they.

Suddenly – he was there. He showed us the way. And suddenly – he was gone. An angel in Venice.

# Chapter 5

## Such an Irritable Bowel!

"I have an irritable bowel, and it's hurting a lot. Please lay your hand on it!"

* * *

I can still remember the pain starting, and that is really weird in itself. One evening I was OK, and the following evening I had a pain. Stomach region, but right of centre, not left. And for some strange reason I noted the day.

After that, I had pain every night. I could relieve it by tucking the thumb of my right hand into my trouser belt, and pulling slightly. In fact, I *needed* to do this or my wife would have become aware of my pain, because it really was very uncomfortable until I pulled on the waistband of my trousers. And she didn't find out about it for quite a long time. (Why did I need to keep it from my wife? – because wives like sending husbands to doctors, and I did not want to go! So I had to prevent her finding out.)

"You've got a pain, haven't you?" she said, as I rapidly withdrew my thumb one evening. But it was no good – she had seen it.

She asked me how long I had had the pain, and having noted when it had started, I could state categorically, "Seventeen months."

So a doctor's appointment was arranged, and I duly attended the surgery of my old friend Dr. John Russell-Wells.

He stared at me over his half-moon glasses, and invited me to be examined. Once this had been completed, he led me back to his consulting room, where he stared at me again over those half moon glasses he always wore.

He had spent some little time checking round my tummy, so I thought he would make a profound pronouncement about my condition, and of the treatment required. I held my breath and waited, only to hear him say,

"I think your trousers are a little tight, Barrie." My trousers? Too tight? My tailor had measured me up properly, and who was John to imply there was a problem with my bags? Regardless, I went to a department store and bought two pairs of trousers one size larger – or was it two, or three? – but the pain continued.

\* \* \*

So I was referred to a specialist who carried out tests, the details of which I will spare you lest you are of a squeamish disposition, or have eaten recently.

He eventually showed me into his consulting room and I sat down in front of the desk. He pulled no punches. I had got IBS. IBS? – I thought that was a Tory politician, but apparently it was 'Irritable Bowel Syndrome'. What was the treatment? – tablets. Phew – at least it wasn't surgery, or worse.

And so I was presented with a pile of small boxes of tablets, and instructed to take three tablets a day, and "two extra before you eat one of those curries you cook yourself." I enquired how long I would need to take the tablets, and the consultant used a terrible word. "IBS is *incurable*. You will take the tablets for the rest of your life."

\* \* \*

As a dentist, when I prescribed tablets for a patient, I expected them to take them. But somehow, I myself didn't quite measure up to this ideal, and so when the pain was tolerable, I forgot about the tablets; when the pain was intolerable, I would take one. But there was still pain every day.

It was a month or so since I had had the consultation, and I was at an early morning prayer meeting at our church in a nearby town. But the pain was distracting me, and became worse. Surely this was not the centre of God's will for me?

I was standing next to a man called Colin, and though I did not know him well enough to be familiar with his understanding of healing, I realised that he *was* the man next to me.

"I have an irritable bowel, and it's hurting a lot. Could you please lay your hand on it and command healing in the Name of Jesus?" I asked.

Colin did just that – and the pain continued.

* * *

It was around six weeks later that I paused one day, and realised that I was not in pain, and in fact, had not been so for a few weeks. Moreover, twenty-five years on, I can say that I have never had IBS pain since and never again taken any of the tablets.

* * *

It was some years later and Wendy did not know what to get me for Christmas. We had had our first date on 1st March 2002, several years after the pain from my IBS had left me, and we had married on 1st March 2003, precisely one year later.

"What do I get the man who has everything?" she asked with a wide smile. "A new study!"

A brilliant idea, I thought. A new study – new shelves, new curtains, and the whole room redecorated. What a lovely wife I have. I took the books from my shelves and stacked them in the utility room, and generally prepared my study for the wonderful invasion.

I started emptying my Victorian roll-top desk before pulling it into the centre of the room and covering it with dustsheets. And there, at the back of a drawer in the top left of the desk, was a collection of small boxes. What were they? I pulled them out, and suddenly their identity dawned on me. They were the IBS tablets prescribed years earlier. I blew the dust off them, took them to the toilet and flushed them away. They were years out of date anyway.

\* \* \*

At the time of writing, it must be around twenty-five years since Colin prayed for me, asking that the power of God might come upon me and heal me. No more pain. No more tablets.

I expect there are those who will claim that the fact that all pain left me shortly after Colin prayed for me is simply a coincidence.

What? – another one? You really must be joking.

# Chapter 6

# Men Who Command the Weather

Fog had been forecast, and fog there certainly was. The control tower radioed Malcolm and told him he would not be taking off that day. However, Colin felt he should pray – and the result was dramatic.

\* \* \*

Malcolm was born in the English county of Norfolk, and on leaving school, trained to be an electrician. It was back in the 1970s, and with increasing inflation and interest rates, public morale was low, and the slogan *'Will the Last Person Leaving Britain Please Turn Out the Light'* was appearing in newspapers, car stickers, and suchlike. Malcolm's boss decided that he would *not* be the last to leave, and bought a one-way ticket to Australia. Malcolm was a young man of 20 at that time, and deciding that he too would launch out – bought his boss's company.

Moira's parents had a stall on Norwich's iconic open-air market, where they sold the freshest of fresh fruit and vegetables to an appreciative and loyal clientele. She and Malcolm had been sweethearts for several years, and around the time he took over the electrical company, they married. And they did so in style, in St. John's Roman Catholic cathedral in the centre of Norwich.

Now at the helm of the business, Malcolm displayed rare business acumen, and after branching out into general building, soon had a portfolio of properties he let out to tenants, as well an aeroplane and a flying school. He needed 750 hours of flying experience in order to gain his commercial flying licence, which could prove expensive. Every 3-hour flight to Le Touquet cost £100 in fuel, but by inviting three friends to join him for the trip at £25 each, and claiming a fuel rebate of £23.50, our resourceful Malcolm's 3-hour flight cost him £1.50!

Moira was friendly with a number of girls, and they would meet up regularly. "What did you do at the weekend?" was the usual small talk. "Went clubbing," said Karen. "Went out for an Indian," said Amanda, whilst Amy looked glum and said, "Stayed at home." "What about you, Moira?" they enquired. She paused, and tried to sound matter-of-fact as she replied, "Malcolm flew us down to Alderney in the Channel Isles, for tea with a friend, and then we continued on to Jersey. We dropped in at Le Touquet for lunch on the way back." Silence! After a week or two, her standard answer to the enquiry was "Not much."

So what does such a successful businessman do in his spare time? Well, one thing that Malcolm did was to wander into the showroom of an upmarket car dealer, and browse. For Malcolm, this was destined to be a life-changing experience.

"Can I help you?" enquired the pleasant proprietor with a disarming smile. Malcolm explained that he was just killing a little time, and was soon engaged in conversation with Graham, who owned the showroom. He mentioned his building company, aeroplane and flying school, while Graham mentioned Mercedes, Jaguar and Rolls Royces.

It was only days later when Malcolm received a phone call from Graham. He was a member of a businessmen's fellowship in the city, and he and a few others were going to a dinner elsewhere in the UK. Could Malcolm fly them there? Malcolm's diary was clear that day, and he duly flew the men to a city around two hundred miles away, and brought them back the next morning. Before long, this became a fairly regular occurrence. The conversation amongst his five passengers was unusual to Malcolm. "What is Jesus doing in your life?" and "God has been really speaking to me," were words that Malcolm heard quite often these days. Coming back from the dinners, the conversations were more interesting still. "That man with arthritis who could hardly walk – he was leaping all over the place. Did you see him?" "I prayed for a fellow who wanted to be filled with the Spirit, and he just crashed out. Lay there like he was dead. Just like Paul on the Damascus road." Malcolm listened, and considered.

Then Malcolm went a step further, and started entering the restaurant towards the close of their meetings. People, both men and women, were walking to the front of the room and being prayed for by the speaker and other businessmen. Some would cry out "I'm healed," whilst others would fall to the floor. Malcolm watched – and considered.

And then there was the fog. Malcolm had flown five men in his six-seater aircraft to North Wales, using the airfield at RAF Valley. They arrived, and the dinner had been as usual – people testifying to their lives having been changed by Jesus, people being healed following prayer, people on the floor, people leaping for joy. Just the usual! The next morning, the weather forecast was fog, but the guys had prevailed upon Malcolm to take them to the airfield where they boarded the plane.

The control tower radioed Malcolm and told him there was insufficient visibility due to the fog, and that it was forecast to remain all day. Malcolm explained to his passengers, but Colin spoke up, saying that as a farmer, he needed to get home in order to do what was required on the farm. He suggested they pray, as he had done so on his farm, and on occasions the rain had stopped over the field he was harvesting while pouring down on the surrounding fields. He had seen the weather change when he had prayed on many occasions. He said that another farmer friend called Tony, that Malcolm also knew, always prayed for the right weather for whatever he needed on his farm. "Jesus has all authority in heaven and on earth, and he has given that authority to his children. Now, let's take authority over this fog – in Jesus' mighty Name!" said Colin.

He immediately went into prayer, commanding in Jesus' Name that the fog lift as he needed to be back on the farm. Around fifteen minutes later, the fog lifted, the control tower radioed the all-clear, and Malcolm took off, nosing up into a clear blue sky.

Once home, he phoned RAF Valley to thank them for their help in landing and take-off, as this was his usual practice. "You're the lucky one," they told him with a chuckle. "The fog unexpectedly lifted, and we gave you clearance to take off, which you did. But twenty minutes later the fog descended again for the rest of the day, just like the forecast said, and we are still closed now."

So much answered prayer, from people's lives being changed, to sicknesses being healed, to the weather dramatically changing. No wonder that one night in Bristol Malcolm surrendered his life to Jesus, and found that he was changed forever. Some years later he found himself president of the Businessmen's Fellowship whose members he had flown to dinners. Malcolm now prayed for the sick and saw them healed – and was a strength and encouragement to me personally at a time of great need. Now Malcolm and Moira are part of the church, *Liberty!*, of which Wendy and I are a part. And if there is one man who very strongly encourages us to pray about problems and needs, that man is Malcolm, who has seen God at work so much.

It was just after the Falklands War with Argentina that Malcolm was asked by a local Christian businessman if he would fly to RAF Northolt and pick up Louis Palau, an Argentinian evangelist, and bring him to Norwich where he was to speak at a Billy Graham Crusade meeting the next day. "Sorry – there must be 24 hours notice, and he must be

*British.*" was the reply from the rather curt, cut-glass accented Ministry man at the airport described as 'the hub of Britain's military flying operations'. Louis Palau was an Argentinian, and Argentina was still seen as *the* enemy in the UK – surely this situation was impossible. Malcolm phoned John, the president of the local Full Gospel Businessmen's Fellowship at the time and he and others prayed. Before long, a titled gentleman and household name was on the phone. "It's OK," he said. "Just fly down and bring him here." So Malcolm did!

But life has not been without real challenges and traumas for Malcolm and Moira. It was on Malcolm's birthday in February 2004 that their son Neal, started feeling quite ill. He had given his life to Jesus as a boy, and more recently had spent time helping build an orphanage in Ghana. Now he was diagnosed with terminal cancer that was already significantly advanced. He had bought a house, and proceeded to bring his wedding forward, and married. That August he rapidly lost weight, and the doctor said he would die well before Christmas. A friend from church, called Murray Norman, went round to their home and, laying hands on Neal, prayed the Lord would heal him. Almost immediately, Neal started putting weight on, and not only enjoyed Christmas, but went away on holiday with Malcolm and Moira. Having given his life to Jesus, and being absolutely secure in that, he told his parents that if he continued in his healing, he was happy with that, but should he die, he knew where he was going, and there was no problem whatsoever – he would be with Jesus.

A whole year had passed (and been enjoyed) as Christmas 2005 approached. Suddenly Neal started losing weight again, and passed into the presence of the One he loved in January 2006. There was hardly a dry eye amongst colleagues who had worked with him at the local University hospital, and he is one of a very few to have a memorial stone laid in his honour in the grounds of the Norfolk and Norwich Hospital at Colney.

A few years later Malcolm started to feel really ill. The diagnosis in 2008 was a tumour on a kidney, with secondaries filling his lungs. He was continually coughing, and had half a kidney removed – and much prayer. He hoped for the best and prepared for the worst, building a house of modest proportions for Moira, his widow to be. But today, seven years on, he has been pronounced healed and fit, and finding their home rather small for the two of them, is preparing to build a larger place where they can enjoy the years ahead.

Malcolm and Moira are grateful to the doctors, nurses and NHS who have cared for them and their family so splendidly over the years, but above all else, they give thanks to Jesus, from whom all healing ultimately flows. Their son had an extra year of quality life, and Malcolm himself is enjoying life when all medical evidence pointed to him no longer being here.

And he often tells us the story of the fog at RAF Valley, where Colin took authority over the weather – and they nosed up into a clear blue sky!

# Chapter 7

# Just a Few Miracles

Three radiographers looked at the X-ray of Stuart's arm, diagnosed a fracture, and it was put in plaster. Then God stepped in!

\* \* \*

Why was it that some of the people in our church could give messages in prophecy and in tongues and interpretations, whereas I could only preach? I wanted to 'move in the gifts' in the way I found described in chapters twelve and fourteen of Paul's first letter to the Corinthians. After a Sunday evening meeting at which the two or three people who seemed especially fluent in prophecy had taken to the floor and let rip for around five to ten minutes each, and at which others of us were encouraged to 'launch out', I returned home with more than a degree of despondency.

Sitting in an armchair in the corner of our bedroom, which was one of those snug places where I liked to withdraw in order to pray, I had a bit of a rant at God. Why were these other men so gifted? Why give *them* the messages? Were they really speaking from heaven? Why not me? Was I being overlooked by God in all this? And so on – rant, rant, rant.

And then, as I ran out of rant and sat quietly, I felt the Lord speak to my heart. It seemed so clear, but could it really be true?

"Barrie, one day you will prophesy like the others, but in the meantime you must be satisfied with healing a few sick folk and working a few miracles."

Really? Little old me? And as I continued to sit silently in the presence of God, I felt he showed me that three people in our church who would be at the next Sunday evening meeting, had something wrong – one was a sickness, one a financial problem, and one something wrong with their car.

The following Sunday evening meeting, I waited until the usual chaps had finished prophesying, and then asked if I could say something. I recounted what I felt the Lord had said to me, and asked if there were three people who identified with my 'words of knowledge'. Six hands went up – two for each category. OK, so there were two for each instead of one. I was just a learner with regard to hearing God, and still am. People gathered round each person, and prayed for them, while I ran from person to person, making sure I laid my hand on each as well as praying for them.

I assumed that they would have their need met by God, and that each would phone me to let me know, so I went home and sat by the telephone. Nothing! An hour or so later there was still nothing, so I got on with my evening.

The following Sunday I arrived at church in good time and stood where people could see me, so that they could come and tell me about their answered prayers from the previous Sunday evening. But no-one did. After a while, I went and sat down with Wendy. I decided that praying for the sick and people with needs was not for me.

\* \* \*

A fortnight later Wendy and I went walking in Dovedale in central England, and it was while we were there that I felt the Lord direct me quite strongly to Matthew 7:34, where we are told that to build one's life on a firm foundation,

we need to *do* what Jesus said. Not just believe, or agree with
– but *do*!

\* \* \*

Back home again, we went to church the following Sunday,
and I asked the elders if I could share what I felt the Lord
had said to me, and explained to the church that if the
Lord really had said that, then people should get healed and
receive miracles if I prayed for them. Suddenly it seemed
like half the church was standing up and walking towards
the back of the building where I said I would stand. I called
out to Wendy to come and help me pray for people, and
for a season, it seemed as if almost everyone we prayed for
received a miracle.

A lady with a congested chest ran to the front of the
church *shouting* that she could breath easily again. A lady
Wendy prayed for was hit by the power of God and crashed to
the floor as God got to work on her. Children came running
over and stared, and one said, "Is she dead?" So many people
seemed to be healed, or have needs met.

And the sceptics would no doubt say "Coincidence",
"Coincidence", "Coincidence", "Coincidence", "Coincidence",
"Coincidence", "Coincidence", "Coincidence"....

\* \* \*

Stuart arrived at the church one morning with his arm in
plaster. He had fallen over in the snow and been taken to
Cromer Hospital where three radiographers had X-rayed him,
and a fracture had been diagnosed. His arm had been set in
plaster. At a certain point in the service, people were invited
to go to the back of the church where Wendy and I would
pray for them. Stuart rose from his seat and made his way
towards us. My faith was not high, probably because I
know how inadequate I am of myself, even though I realise it

is God who does the miracles. 'Maybe he'll say he has backache', I kidded myself, unable to take my eyes off his plaster.

"I've broken my arm, and I'd like the Lord to heal it," said Stuart, predictably.

I laid my hands on his plaster, and asked that the power of God might come upon him and bring about healing. In fact, several other people, probably with more faith than me, had already done so when Stuart had first arrived at church that morning. Stuart thanked me and went back to his seat.

\* \* \*

The following Sunday, Stuart walked into church without plaster. I stared at him. Why am I surprised when God heals somebody in response to prayer? And why am I surprised when God does *not* heal somebody in response to prayer? Do others suffer from this strange condition?

"Where's the plaster?" I asked Stuart.

"I went to have it changed, because they said they would need to after a week or so," said Stuart, "and when they took the plaster off, they said that my arm wasn't broken after all."

I asked Stuart about the X-rays they had taken, and he said that when the plaster came off, they looked at his arm and said it did not look broken to them, and so they sent him for more X-rays. The result was that the arm was *not* broken. I asked what explanation they had given about the first X-rays that showed it broken, but Stuart had not asked. So we simply rejoiced that after prayer, the arm was sound again. Which was very good news for Stuart because he needed his arm in order to carry out his work.

Isn't it amazing – a man breaks his arm, another person prays to God that he will be healed, and he is. And there are those who will say, "Coincidence"!

\* \* \*

There was an interesting sequel to the story of Stuart's broken arm. Some months later, we had planned a holiday in Indonesia, but felt that we would rather 'give our holiday to God'. It was Wendy's idea really, but I thought it was truly inspired. We talked to our church leaders about it and asked where they thought we could be useful for a fortnight. They said that 'A' was for Albania and 'B' was for Bulgaria and 'C' was for China and 'D' was for... So Wendy and I sat down and asked the Lord where he would like us to go, and we somehow ended up with four countries – Turkey, China, India, and Mexico. We quickly received information that three of these countries were not for us, which left – Mexico!

The church we went to in Guadalajara, the second city in Mexico, gave us a very nice flat for our stay, and used us in speaking English to people who wanted to learn it, preaching the gospel in the slum areas, playing football with the young boys, and so on. We were a few days into the time when we received a message that a boy in a school had a broken arm, and could we go there at the end of lessons (so not to distract the pupils) and heal the arm. It turned out the pastor there had heard from the pastor back in the UK about Stuart's healed arm.

We arrived at the school at the end of the day, and found that the whole class had stayed behind to 'watch the miracle'. No pressure!

The teacher asked us to explain why we were in Mexico, and after that called the boy with the fractured arm to the front of the class. The arm had been broken – but a year previously. The fracture had been complex, and needed an operation, and this had resulted in it being fixed with pins and plates. There were scars like little ladders running from his wrist to nearly his shoulder. The problem, we were told, was that he could no longer straighten his arm, but had to go through each day with the arm permanently bent. He would like to be able to straighten it and bend it again, please.

If Wendy and I had faith the tenth of the size of a mustard seed, we would have felt a little better than we did. Although I usually expect the Lord to heal people when I lay hands on them and pray for them, I am not God's man of faith and power, like some of the people we read about in the Bible. Wendy and I looked at each other, and then laid our hands on the boy's arm and asked that the power of God might come upon it and bring healing.

Right in front of our eyes, and in front of the class, the arm straightened out. We stared in amazement. I thought it was just a little short of perfectly straight, Wendy gasped and said, "Look what God has done", and Emilio, the ten year old boy beamed at us and said. "The pain has gone. The pain has gone." (We did not know that he had been in pain). At this, the teacher suggested that the class 'give the Lord a round of applause', which they did with great excitement.

Wendy and I have often spoken together, and to others, about what we saw that day, and feel that it was the most remarkable healing miracle that the two of us have personally witnessed. We also heard that one year later Emilio returned to hospital and had the pins and plates removed, as he had perfect healing and perfect function.

To me, it seems so conclusive a miracle, that I am tempted to question the motives of those who argue that it was 'just a coincidence' or 'merely psychosomatic'. Let me tell you a secret – it really was a miracle, because God did it!

# Chapter 8

# Two Frozen Shoulders
# and an Electric Leg

"Can you help me get dressed?" said my wife – an unusual request after several years of marriage, but I duly assisted with slipping things on and slipping things over and doing things up. I'm sure my own clothes are far less complicated!

\* \* \*

It all began in February 2008, when Wendy started squeaking in bed when she turned over. Clearly she was in some discomfort, and the pain was in fact coming from her shoulders. With no exaggeration, she would shout during the night, every night, when she rolled over – and Wendy is not one to complain, ever, about anything. There was also the problem of getting dressed, because she could not lift her arms higher than her shoulders. She assumed it would get better, but the months passed...

It was the spring of 2008 when Mark approached me one morning in the church we attended in a nearby town. Mark was around thirty years of age, and Wendy and I had become really friendly with him when he first came to the church. We had called him 'the son we had never had'. Had I heard that there was an outpouring of the Spirit at a place called Lakeland in Florida? No, I hadn't. He and his wife were thinking of going there. "Wonderful," I said, and told him

I had never been to such a happening, and would love to hear all about it when they returned.

"But we have been praying together about it, and feel that you and Wendy should come with us," he said with a smile. "Well, if you feel that's right for you. Pray about it."

Wow! I had never considered going to 'an outpouring', and the idea sent a tingle through me. Wendy and I looked on the Internet, and found that an evangelist called Todd Bentley had gone to a church at Lakeland to conduct a short mission. However, it seemed like the presence of God had descended on the place, and people started getting miraculously healed, others were 'set free' from conditions and situations that had really prevented them from enjoying life and enjoying God – and people were giving their lives to Christ. So many people were flocking there that the church building would not hold them, and they were now meeting in an aircraft hangar. Todd Bentley himself seemed an unusual character, as he was covered with tattoos. We assumed he had led a colourful life before he came to Christ.

We had booked to go to Venice early in August, and Mark and his wife wanted to go to Florida late August. We prayed about going with them, having first decided that unless we got a clear 'No' from heaven, we were going. We did not hear a 'No' and so we bought tickets and arranged accommodation in a hotel near the site of the meetings.

\* \* \*

It was quite late one evening in Venice, and having had dinner we were preparing for bed when my mobile phone rang. It was Mark. Had I heard? Todd Bentley had stood down from taking meetings at Lakeland. There were rumours of a scandal, and there were a lot less people at the meetings as a result. Did we still want to go?

I explained that there were two reasons I wanted to go. Firstly, I simply wanted to see what *God* was doing, and whether it was Todd Bentley or Uncle Tom Cobbly preaching made little difference to me. Secondly, I wanted to get the hands of the leadership there fairly and squarely on my head, because I had heard that the anointing to heal was transferrable. Nothing to lose and everything to gain – we were still going.

\* \* \*

There were around 500 people there each evening when we arrived in late August. The pastor of Ignite church, Stephen Strader, spoke for a short while most evenings, and we were impressed with the wisdom with which he handled the situation – the regular members feeling confused by the evangelist leaving prematurely, and the rest of us wanting to see God in action.

Most evenings the main speaker was Frank Seamster, a southerner. We loved his preaching, and were encouraged that he did not 'turn on the emotion' or use lots of clichés. People went forward for prayer for healing, but we did not see anything dramatic. However, we heard some testimonies from people who had been at earlier meetings, and who were undeniably healed from serious conditions.

We sat there one evening, listened to the speaker and watched people go forward for prayer. Then we returned to our hotel, and after a glass of wine, went to bed. The next morning, Wendy found that both her arms were healed. No pain at all, whatever she did with them. The day before – lots of pain. Every day from February through to the day before in August – lots of pain. Suddenly – no pain.

The following evening we were sitting in the meeting when Mark, who was on my left, turned to me and whispered, "I've got electricity going through my leg!"

I asked him what he meant, and he said that there was the sensation of electricity running up and down his leg. Once the meeting was over, I asked him to explain further.

Mark told me that he had injured his leg eighteen months earlier and had been unable to go jogging in the mornings. He wondered whether the sensation was the Lord healing him. It certainly sounded like it. So when he got up the next morning, Mark went to the jogging machine in the hotel gymnasium – and jogged a mile and a half. He has had no trouble since.

I had tinnitus, and at times in the meeting asked the Lord if he would heal me. Nothing happened. However, I did have a strange experience. During the praise times, there was a good beat to the music and I moved into the aisle and started to dance. I do this to express what is in my heart with regard to what the Lord has done in my life. He's done a lot, and I truly feel like dancing for joy when I consider it. So sometimes I dance! I had the sensation of liquid dripping onto my head, and assuming it was condensation from the high roof due to the air conditioning (this *was* Florida), moved. But it happened again, and I moved a time or two, and then just accepted it.

I remarked to Mark later about the dripping, and said I thought they needed to adjust the air conditioning. But Mark had avoided it. In fact, so had his wife and so had Wendy. And everybody else I mentioned it to had the same story – no dripping. I pondered over this for some while, because I was definitely dripped on, and my best guess is that the Lord was anointing me in some manner, and demonstrating it with a dripping on my head.

\* \* \*

"Will all those leaving tomorrow please come forward so that we can pray for you," said Stephen Strader. I really wanted the anointing they had in those meetings, and together with Wendy and our friends, went forward to the front. As they laid their hands upon us, the power of God hit us and we collapsed on the floor. I do not know why God does it that way, but simply accept that he knows best.

There was another call for leaders to go forward for prayer, and Mark gave me a dig in the ribs and suggested I get out there for a second helping. I was not sure about being a leader, as our church at home was very clear about their leadership team, and who was in it – and Wendy and I were not. "Get out there," said Mark. "It's God who makes people leaders. Get out there." So we went and received our second helping, or in my case, probably my third.

\* \* \*

We had been home around a fortnight, and I was clearing the ditch around the side of our home where there is a lane. A man was walking his dog along the lane, and I had met him once before briefly in the village, and remembered his name as Pete.

"Hello Pete. How are you and your dog today?" I enquired.

"Not good," replied Pete. "I have been feeling unwell, and the doctor has just told me. I have leukaemia."

I leant on my shovel. "Pete," I said. "Wendy and I have just returned from Florida where there have been meetings accompanied by an outpouring of God's Spirit. The leaders there have laid their hands on us, and the power to heal is said by some to be transferrable. Please let me lay my hands on you and I believe the Lord will heal you."

Pete had looked rather pale, but as I spoke he went as white as a sheet, and his eyes opened like tea-plates.

"No thanks," said Pete, and he started running slowly backwards whilst still facing me and keeping his wide-open eyes fixed on me. "Actually, I am feeling a lot better already." And he ran up the lane and back into the village.

Instant healing? I think 'instant terror', indicating that I needed to learn better how to approach people.

But both before and after visiting Ignite Church at Lakeland I have seen quite a lot of people healed through the laying on of hands and prayer. I suppose some people have to call these healings 'coincidences' – rather like Wendy being completely healed of all pain after suffering every day for six months, and like Mark being completely healed of his running injury, after being unable to jog for eighteen months.

But actually – it's our miracle working God!

# Chapter 9

# The Curious Case of the Constipated Cat!

"Your cat is really quite poorly," said William Oakes, our local friendly vet. "If she becomes constipated like this again, I think that will be the end." Two weeks later she was once more seriously gummed up.

*  *  *

"Watch out for dogs. They bite you." I was around four years of age at the time, but I can still hear my mother's words of warning. And I was to be especially careful of a small white dog called 'Spot'. He had already bitten a child in our village.

Some decades later, I could happily have sat in the back of a truck with a shotgun, polishing off almost anything smaller than a horse, and with four legs. Pets – what was the point? They did not lay eggs, you couldn't milk them and you couldn't eat them. A waste of time.

*  *  *

It was February 1993 and we had almost continual sub-zero temperatures in our home county of Norfolk. We would sit by the log fire in our sitting room, gazing out at the hoar frost adorning the weeping birches. Outside the front door was a patio, bordered on two sides by shrubberies. Having donned a warm coat before venturing out with my camera in order to capture something of the sheer beauty of our glistening ice-laced trees, I noticed movement behind a shrub to my left. As I approached, it gave a winsome little mew.

We really had no idea what to do with a stray cat, especially an almost frozen stray cat, but I used to watch some television in those days (I had time then, before I retired) and had seen adverts for cat food. Having learnt from these ads that nine out of ten cats had a preference for a particular brand (it was the ads for that brand which furnished me with this invaluable information), I purchased a few tins, placed a saucer of chicken-based mush under a Weigela and retreated. Later that evening I retrieved the empty saucer, and repeated the exercise the following day.

My wife was not well at that time, unable to leave our home and spending most of her time sitting beside the fire knitting. On returning from the surgery on day three, I was not surprised to find the cat asleep beside her on the sofa.

We were not too sure how to look after a cat, and felt that if we were to have one as a pet, we might well choose a different breed. We phoned the cat rescue centre for advice, took it in, missed it, phoned to see if we could have it back only to find that firstly, it now had somebody else's name on it, and secondly, it was pregnant.

\* \* \*

A fortnight later we returned to the house with a Siamese kitten. We had perused cat books, scanned advertisements in our local paper, and driven out to Ormesby St. Margaret to select Bathsheba. Her name was actually unpronounceably Siamese, but Bathsheba was her given name in our home. I had not realised how deeply one could love a kitten, and was totally smitten. But what if she should ever have an accident, or become seriously ill? How would we cope emotionally with losing her? And so we added a second Siamese to our family, Solomon. I jokingly called him our 'spare', but he was as much a part of our family as Bathsheba. And then, just before his fourth birthday, Solomon got in the way of a car, and left a gaping hole in our family and our hearts. We wept every day for a week, and after around three months, were joined by another Siamese kitten, Arabella.

Arabella rarely ventured beyond the borders of our country garden. As the years passed, she had a tendency to pick up respiratory infections, whilst Bathsheba started going deaf as she approached her teens. We were towards the end of a walking holiday in our beloved Dovedale when we received a phone call to inform us that Arabella had passed away, quietly curled up on the lap of the proprietor of the local cattery.

Bathsheba was fourteen now, which I was told was a very respectable age for a Siamese. She was an old lady, and at times lost her appetite and seemed to be suffering from constipation. We took her to the vet on several occasions and he relieved the situation. And then poor Bathsheba really seemed to go downhill, moping around, eating virtually nothing, and passing nothing. The vet was wonderful as ever, and after attending to her in his surgery, explained that certain muscles and processes were not really working any more.

"Your cat is really quite poorly," said Mr. Oakes. "If she becomes constipated like this again, I think that will be the end." Two weeks later she was once more seriously gummed up.

Bathsheba had her own room in the house, where there was no sensor to trigger the security system, and her own cat flap to enable her to enter and exit at will. But she neither entered nor exited; she just lay on her rug and slept. A terminal trip to the vet seemed inevitable.

When my wife suddenly left me for a man she had met online, it had been more than a shock to find myself alone in the house back in August 2001 – continuing to cook as I had for the previous eighteen years or so, but now also undertaking my washing and ironing as well. Plus the grief. Then Wendy had come into my life on 1st March 2002, and we had married on 1st March 2003. She had so selflessly left her cats in the care of a neighbour, and truly adopted mine. The years had passed, and now we discussed Bathsheba, and prayed about the situation. But could we seriously pray for pets? For animals?

Wendy had left for work, managing a nursing home in North Norfolk, and I was about to leave for my surgery. I went through to Bathsheba's room where she was languishing on her rug. She half-opened her eyes and gazed at me. Surely the end was nigh.

I felt a sudden surge of faith, and stepping forward, extended my right hand towards her and said aloud, "May the power of God come upon you and bring healing to whatever is wrong." She gazed at me for a few seconds, closed her eyes and appeared to fall asleep as I shut the door and proceeded to the surgery.

\* \* \*

I usually managed to drive home for a short break at lunchtime, and hopefully a snack. I parked the car in the garage, disarmed the security system and walked through to the kitchen. Bathsheba – I should check her first. She was clearly unwell, and though not eating, would appreciate company and comfort. I passed through the hall and opened the door to her room.

Urrrggghhhh! Stench! Worse! I stepped back, only to hear the Siamese cries of my favourite (and only) cat demanding food. I stepped forward and shouted "Hallelujah!", and surveyed the soiled rug and surrounding area. But there was no time to clean up her room – this cat was hungry and needed to be fed.

Wendy is the great cleaner upper, and later that day did not take too long to make the room habitable again. I went to the front of the church the following Sunday and shared what had happened. "Too much information," the pastor's wife said to Wendy with the hint of a smile.

Bathsheba? She found her appetite again, along with her capacity to pass what was required, and continued with us for a further two years, enjoying good health until she suddenly deteriorated and departed for a better place.

I have no doubt that sceptics will say that Bathsheba's dramatic recovery following prayer was just another coincidence. No problem – but many of us know better!

# Chapter 10

# One in a Zillion

When a church meets together, there are various components to the overall meeting. More traditional churches might call it a 'service'. One of these components is praise, another is worship, another prayer and so on. But one important component is often left out by the more traditional churches, and that is the one found in 1 Corinthians 14:26.

In modern versions of the Bible, we read in this verse that, 'When you meet together, each one of you has...' And the verse goes on to give some examples of what people might bring to the meeting – a psalm (probably a 'song' today), a teaching (maybe a scripture, or something that's happened, from which they have learnt something), a message in tongues or an interpretation of a tongue (or another of the gifts of the Spirit that we read about in 1 Corinthians 12:7-10), and a revelation (something that the Spirit has shown us recently)

At our church called *Liberty!*, we try to do that. We encourage one another to be aware of these things, and if something new is learnt, or if the Lord has done something special in one's life during the week, to come to the meeting prepared to share. And in our meetings we try to be aware of the prompting of the Spirit for people to give a message in tongues, or a prophecy, or any of the other gifts of the Spirit. In larger meetings it is impossible for each person to contribute in this way, but we should all come prepared, both those with responsibility for overseeing, and individual members of the congregation.

So we do not come to the meeting determined to contribute, and nor do we come determined *not* to. But we do come *prepared* to share.

Some months ago, around eighteen of us had gathered together one Sunday morning. Barry was always with us, and indeed, had been with us from the outset. Vincent felt a great affinity for the way the Lord had led the development and style of our church and meetings, and though part of another church some miles away, would visit us periodically. As usual, we had asked the Holy Spirit to come amongst us. There was a great time of praise and worship, and a real sense of the presence of the Spirit of God with us. One or two of the gifts of the Holy Spirit were manifest, and some people prayed out loud.

Barry said that the Lord had shown him something in the Scriptures, and he would like to share it with us. Vincent said he also had something to contribute. So Barry opened his Bible, and read a verse from the New Testament. He told us what he had learnt from it, so that we could too. Vincent then read his verse, from a book in the Old Testament, and explained what he had seen in it. I thought that both verses were rather obscure, but also that the Lord had clearly led them to their respective verses and shown them what they had just shared, which was very practical and relevant.

The Bible I was using had cross-references in the margin. What is a cross-reference? It is a reference to another Bible verse, or verses, where the same theme or subject is found. Most verses have several cross-references to similar verses. Out of interest I looked to see what cross-references there were beside Barry's verse. There was only one – and it was Vincent's verse. And beside Vincent's verse, predictably, was Barry's verse. (I wish I had made a note of the verses)

Is that remarkable? Firstly, Barry and Vincent hardly know each other, and so the connection between the verses did not spring from any conversation the two might have had. Barry only meets Vincent when he comes to a meeting, which at that time was approximately once every three months. Secondly, each of them had felt directed to their respective verse whilst on their own with God during the previous week. It was not a case of one sharing his verse, and the other recalling a similar verse.

Thirdly, there are 31,173 verses in the Bible. In my Bible, neither verse had any other cross-reference. Just the two – out of 31,173. I wonder what the mathematical probability was of that happening by chance.

You've probably guessed that I am convinced that God was making his presence known to us through that incident. It was a miracle. But some people would say it was just a coincidence!

\* \* \*

At another of our meetings, two people each said they had a scripture they would like to read at the start of our time. "After you," said one. "No, you read yours," said the other. We decided that Pete would read his scripture, and Karen would read hers later if it fitted in. Pete read his scripture, which seemed really appropriate. "That's from Job chapter 5," exclaimed Karen. I was quite amazed that Karen knew that, as I have no clear idea of the actual text in Job chapter 5.

"How do you know that?" I enquired.

"Because that is the verse that the Lord gave me for this morning," said Karen.

This time it was well more than a 1 in 31,173 chance. In fact, the chance of two people having that same scripture was far more remote than 1 in 31,173. To me, it was one in a zillion – an act of God. But some people would call it a coincidence!

\* \* \*

On innumerable occasions, someone in the meeting has prayed out loud, and someone else has followed with, "I was going to pray that!"

On many occasions in our meetings, someone has spoken words of prophecy. (Prophecy within the context of a church meeting is not usually predictive, but simply a message from God to 'edify, exhort, or to comfort'. So says the Spirit through 1 Corinthians 14:3. Some would phrase it as 'to build you up, buck you up, or cheer you up'.) Following the person's prophecy, someone else has said, "I've had those words going round in my head for the last ten minutes."

Some people would call that a coincidence!

\* \* \*

I have already mentioned that I am a member of an international fellowship of Christian businessmen. In our local city of Norwich, we have monthly dinners at a hotel. We try to invite people who are non-believers, and have a speaker who 'tells his story'. What is the speaker's story? Some are respectable businessmen who have lived decent lives before coming to Christ and finding real fulfilment, whilst others have a history of drink, tobacco, drugs, crime and prison before finding that Jesus sets people free from addictions. Generally they testify of physical and emotional healing and other miracles.

We had a speaker not so long ago, who had come to Christ, and enjoyed a whole new life. He was successful as a young man in business, but after changing employment, tumbled into depression and felt far from God. He was despairing, and as time passed concluded that there really was no hope for him. He decided to try attending church one final time, and the preacher spoke on the Bible verse 2 Chronicles 20:15, which reads 'The battle is not yours, but God's.' He realised that only the Lord could get him back on his feet again, but needed reassurance.

On returning home, his mother told him that she had been so concerned about him, that she had stayed in her room all morning in order to pray for him. She said that the same verse kept coming into her mind, to the extent that she had written it down for him. She handed him a piece of paper with the scripture on it. The verse? 2 Chronicles 20:15. Our speaker had felt so tremendously encouraged at the way the Lord had brought the same scripture to his attention twice, that he rededicated his life to Jesus and moved ahead confidently, into a whole new future. 31, 173 verses. The same verse *twice* that morning? It's a one in a zillion chance again. I call that another absolute miracle. But some people would say that it's yet another coincidence.

* * *

The sceptics have to call these things coincidences. Always, every time, every one of them. Well, they would, wouldn't they! This is not a proof for the existence of God, but just an encouragement for those who know him anyway. And for those who do not, they are pointers. The Lord does not give us proofs, but evidence, indicators, pointers – and an invitation.

Many coincidences at a zillion to one chance each? Come on! It's much more reasonable to accept the One who is so clearly reaching out to us. Do so!

# Chapter 11

# Landslide!

"Lord, if we were wrong to invite this man, please show us – or even prevent him from coming."

But Mike and I were totally bowled over by what happened next!

\* \* \*

It had been a year or so earlier that Mark Botherington (not his real name) had contacted me on Facebook.

"Hey, I'm a member of the FGB – the Full Gospel Businessmen's Fellowship. How are you?" said the man from the north of England. "Pretty good," I responded.

So we became friends. Well, Facebook friends. Mark saw that I was an author, and told me that he was too. Mark saw that I spoke at FGB dinners, and told me that he did too.

\* \* \*

"When are you going to invite me to speak at your FGB dinner? You are president, aren't you?" wrote Mark on my Facebook messenger.

I asked him where he had spoken before, and he reeled off a string of FGB dinners. But he was *so* keen to speak at our dinner, and sell his book to us. Keen? – almost pushy.

And he kept asking, "When are you going to invite me? When can I come and speak?" I weakened. Lesson – don't be like Barrie! When the warning light starts flashing (and it was), pay attention.

Eventually I asked Mark when he was free, and he was duly booked in to speak at our FGB dinner late winter 2014. Around a month before the dinner, we started publicising the event, largely through the Internet. 'Mark Botherington, bricklayer and author, will be speaking at our next dinner. In addition to being in the building industry, Mark is also an author and has had a life-changing experience of the living God. Come and hear him.'

I have changed a few of the details.

\* \* \*

Before long people started booking to come to the dinner to hear Mark. But other people started to get in touch too.

"We had him at our dinner, and all he did was promote *himself*."

"He came and spoke at our dinner, and did a really hard sell on his book."

"He came to us. Quite a few people bought his book, and then found the pages were out of order."

But we heard from some other people that he had spoken well at their dinners, though he did wave his book around a lot.

\* \* \*

I sent an email to Mark, asking him if he could give me any references with regard to his previous speaking engagements. At this, Mr. Botherington became a little angry, and told me that he was answerable to no man, but to Jesus only. OK, if there was ever an indication that a man was rebellious, surely that was it. And then he gave me the name of a man in the FGB, a man who had responsibility for a large region, and said that he had spoken widely in that area.

The man whose name he gave me was in fact, a respected member and officer in the FGB. I telephoned him, and he told me that Mark had been to his region and spoken several times. He was somewhat self-promoting, but could also win to Christ people that others could not reach. He said that he would have him to speak again – and that was quite a recommendation.

\* \* \*

I telephoned Mike, our FGB regional director, and we discussed it. We did not know which way to turn, and so we prayed and asked the Lord that, if I was wrong to invite Mark, he would either show us clearly, or prevent him from coming.

There was further communication with Mark, and unlike other speakers, he did not want to stay at our home overnight, but had already booked in at the hotel where we held our dinners, at his own expense. He was not driving to us like most speakers, but had decided to come by train.

"I might want to evangelise people in the bar after the meeting," he explained. "And there is a lady near there who has read my book and who wants to meet me. Nothing wrong with that, is there mate?"

It seemed wrong to cancel him, and wrong to continue with him. Mike and I prayed again.

\* \* \*

The day of the dinner arrived. It was arranged that I should meet Mark at the station and run him to the hotel where the dinner was being held, and where he had booked in overnight.

"I'll be at the station by 5 p.m.," he said. "You can run me to the hotel, and then I'll come down for the dinner and speak to the people."

It was not the most convenient of arrangements for me, but as president, I wanted to serve the fellowship and see that everything ran as smoothly as possible.

\* \* \*

Everything was prepared, with our banner and promotional literature in the boot ('trunk' -USA) of the car.

"I'll see you there," I said to Wendy. "I'll set out for the station at 4.30 p.m. and remain at the hotel for the meeting. It's too far to come home again after dropping Mark off there"

It was 3.30 p.m. Suddenly, my mobile blew a raspberry at me to let me know that a text had arrived. 'Can't make it mate,' read the text from Mark Botherington. 'There's been a landslide in front of my train and it can't get through. I can go round by Nottingham, but I would not arrive until tomorrow.'

\* \* \*

How great is our God! How amazing he is! How often do you get a landslide blocking the path of a train in the UK? And how often following a prayer like that?

So Mark never arrived, and to this day has not contacted me again. We were left without a speaker for the evening, but – they had not really heard *me* before. Also, I had no expenses for the fellowship. I simply spoke and told people my story, and offered to pray for any people who were in need. And Wendy and I were there until late. Very late.

\* \* \*

It was the only time we asked the Lord to prevent a speaker arriving if I had made a bad choice. It was the only time a speaker was prevented from coming by a landslide blocking the path of a train – but with no casualties!

A sign, a wonder, an act of the living God? And some would call it a coincidence? Come on!

# Chapter 12

## *Not* Them *in Our Home!*

"I'm surprised at you," said the man walking his dog through our village. "I didn't think you'd have *them* in your home. Don't you know what they are?"

\* \* \*

It had all started early in 2011, when a slightly warmer sun started rising a little higher in the sky, cock pheasants were ruffling their colourful plumage and strutting round the now fallow barley field opposite our cottage, to win the hearts of the females of the species, whilst male lapwings were tumbling through the air in order to captivate the attention of their lady loves. I needed to lose weight, and diet and exercise were the way ahead. So I started walking, and talking around the village where I live. This was a multipurpose activity; the exercise took off a few pounds and enhanced muscle tone, and also brought some of the lovely characters from our village across my path and into my life. Some of these were people of faith, no doubt, but spreading the Christian message by telling folk what Jesus has done for me has been part of my life since Barrie the atheist became Barrie the born-again Christian back in October 1965. And so I asked the Lord for opportunities to share my faith in our village.

I made conversation with those I met. "What breed of dog is that?" I asked dog walkers, and "Have you heard the forecast?" to those without a canine companion. Sometimes my faith came up in conversation, but usually not. For me, it has to 'come up naturally in conversation', and as that generally did not happen, I simply enjoyed the company and conversation of whoever I bumped into. But every week or two I found myself speaking to someone about my journey from atheism, or of examples of answered prayer.

And then in summer 2012, God stepped in, and brought a certain property to my attention. I had never seen anybody there, though it was clearly lived in. And occasionally there would be a Jaguar car standing on the drive – but never on Sunday.

Prayer has been an integral part of my life since 1965. I prayed while I walked the village, and took time out regularly to get alone with God. It was during one of these times that I felt the Lord calling me to speak to the people in the bungalow with the Jaguar car. I will not go into great detail here, but I felt he showed me the home and he then showed me the day and time to visit them.

\* \* \*

With my heart beating a little more strongly than usual, I rang the doorbell and waited. After what seemed an age, a shape appeared behind the frosted glass and the door opened.

"Yes?" said the tall casually dressed fellow who filled the doorway.

I explained that I lived on the far side of the village, also drove a Jaguar car, and believed that the God of the Bible had directed me to speak to him about my faith.

Ken (not his real name) was a Jehovah's Witness, and it must have been strange for him to find a stranger on *his* doorstep telling him about *their* faith. In fact, not only did I tell him about my faith, I also gave him a Christian magazine for his attention later. I suggested he consider what I had said, and that we meet again sometime. Maybe he would like to come to a Full Gospel dinner?

Two weeks later I received an email from the gentleman telling me that he was clear about the significance of the 144,000, of blood, and of anniversaries. Therefore, he explained, there was nothing to be gained in meeting again. But the God I seek to serve had other plans!

* * *

For some months we had been planning to have some major alterations carried out to our home. We regularly had in excess of twenty people to supper, and our dining room was small. We often had several of our six daughters and many grandchildren (nineteen at the time of writing, though a few less in 2012) to stay with us, and could do with more than five bedrooms. So we bit the bullet and decided to have two internal walls demolished, and six rooms refurbished. Well, if my study was to be incorporated into a new dining room, I would need a new study. If one of the utility rooms was to become my new study, we would need a new utility room. If the wine store which doubled as a bike room was to become a new utility room... I think we were fortunate to have only six rooms refurbished.

It was late summer 2012 and within a few weeks a builder we knew had arranged to commence the work and finish it all within a month. And for two of those weeks we would be away, exploring the Atacama Desert in Chile. Suddenly, seeming disaster. The builder was so apologetic, but he was just too busy. These things happen. He was sure we could find someone else. No, he could not think of anyone to recommend.

Wendy was very quiet for a day or so, because as the hostess extraordinaire, she had been particularly excited about the new dining room. And the other rooms. She sat down with a copy of the Yellow Pages, and made a list of five local builders, and then picked up the telephone.

She introduced herself, and said which village we lived in, and then proceeded to explain that we really wanted a substantial amount of work carried out within a four week period in about three weeks time.

"Where exactly do you live?" Each of them asked.

"In the pink house by the crossroads, set back from the road, with a shingle drive," was her reply each time.

"Is that Barrie Lawrence's house?" asked builder number three on her list.

"Yes. Do you know my husband?" she asked. Her question was followed by a pause on the other end of the line.

"Not exactly," said builder number three, "but he walked up *my* drive three weeks ago, and told me all about his faith."

And so it was that the following day Ken found himself walking up *our* drive, to be greeted with a broad smile and the words, "I told you the Lord has really got his hand on your life!"

He walked round the house noting measurements and details in his notebook, and said he would email an estimate and other information to us the next day.

The following afternoon I was driving back from the golf course when there was a 'ping' from my mobile phone. Somehow, I suspected it would be an email from Ken, and I pulled off the road onto the edge of a field. Ken was a partner in a construction company, and they built houses as well as doing smaller alterations and suchlike. His estimate of the cost was in line with three of the other companies. (A fifth company which comprised two large men who kicked walls, paced out lengths of rooms, who kept repeating 'No prob mate', and who Wendy referred to as Bodger and Badger, had dropped out of our 'top four'). We immediately telephoned Ken, who came round to see us. Strangely, his order book, which was usually full for a few months, was totally clear in three weeks time, and remained so for four weeks, after which it was full again. What an amazing coincidence! I remarked that surely this must have been divinely arranged, and Ken smiled.

So the builders arrived, and in fact did so on the day we had asked for. Ken's business partner was a Jehovah's Witness, and the electrician was – guess what? – a Jehovah's Witness. So was the bricklayer, and you can imagine what the decorator was – a Jehovah's Witness. The young man who generally brought in supplies and manned the wheel-barrow? – he was a Jehovah's Witness. So though we were away for two weeks, we had another two weeks when we had a lot of contact with the builders. I explained to the people in our church that except on weekends, we now had wall-to-wall Jehovah's Witnesses in the house, and we prayed that the Lord would give us opportunities to share our faith in the true and living God.

They were such decent people, and we would recommend them as builders to others. Virtually no dust penetrated their sheets and seals, they were polite and punctual, and were extremely considerate. I greeted them each morning, and we would spend a little time in conversation. They said they had not been born-again. They seemed quite amazed at some of our accounts of answered prayer, as if that never happened to them. Which I suppose it did not.

We thought we would ask them round for a celebration supper, but our diary was quite full, and we heard that Jehovah's Witnesses usually declined invitations to the homes of born-again Christians. However, we have invited some of that sect to parties at our home, though we have yet to see any of them come along. We continue to have contact with them, and feel that the hand of God is so clearly on this relationship. But we are not short-term people, and whilst being serious about walking with the Lord, will not try and accelerate matters faster than he decrees.

\* \* \*

It was now early spring 2013, and great cushions of cow parsley were bouncing in the wind along the banks of the lane where we live, and blackthorn blossom was again making a somewhat early appearance in the hedgerows around our garden. Me? I had spring-cleaned the summerhouse and was using it as my prayer room. Prayer? It was more of a rant!

"I thought you were going to give me opportunities to share my faith with people in this village?" I launched into a prayer tirade. "I'm not going to *force* my testimony on them. I'm not someone who can keep bringing it into conversations. You know who I am and what I'm like. Well, you made me, or created me, or whatever. So why no opportunities to share my faith..." and so on and so forth, ad nauseam, ad infinitum.

I put down the Bible I had been reading from, one of two Bibles that live in the summerhouse, and walked out of the small side-gate and strode up the road towards the mill. Walking towards me was a man with a dog, and as I got closer, I recognised John. (Not his real name). He had lived in the village for many years, and I had once invited him to one of our Businessmen's Fellowship's dinners. He had turned down my invitation, explaining that it was not for 'people like me', and I wondered whether he felt he was not a businessman, or whether he had twigged that it was a Christian gathering and perhaps he was wary of such.

"I'm surprised at you," said John. "I didn't think you'd have *them* in your home. Don't you know what they are?"

"What do you mean?" I enquired.

"They're Jehovah's" said John, giving a slightly mischievous smile. "You didn't know that, did you? The builders who have been working on your home. They're Jehovah's."

"You mean that because I'm a Christian you thought I would not employ Jehovah's Witnesses?" I asked.

I proceeded to explain to John how I had been praying, and felt the Lord directing me to a certain house in the village, and how I had rung their doorbell and found they were Jehovah's Witnesses.

"You went up *their* front path and rang their bell?" said John, almost unable to contain his mirth.

So I continued with the story, and how I had given Ken a Christian magazine.

"I love it. I love it," said John. "You gave *them* a magazine!"

"Certainly did," I continued, and explained how Ken really wanted nothing more to do with me, until Wendy had telephoned local builders. "Surely God has got his hand on these people?" I said, as I explained how Ken's diary had a gap just when we needed the work carrying out. I told John of the blessing to us of such considerate workmen, and of all the answered prayer we had experienced at that time. We had been able to tell them of Duane and Cherie and the restored relationship within their family, and of Bob and Sue and the evening's work that was cancelled almost immediately when we prayed about it...

* * *

We have an ongoing relationship with Ken, who has now heard of how my life has been changed by Jesus, and so many of his workforce have heard about the living God who answers prayer. I don't believe the Lord has finished with them yet. He has brought all this about, and I believe it's all to do with his kingdom.

However, I also believe they are frightened of me! They will not come to an FGB dinner, and when I have invited other members of the sect to parties at our home (*not* Christmas), they refuse to come. And more importantly, they do not come to our doorstep – well, only twice in thirty-three years – and others I have invited to come and discuss theology have never arrived.

John used to keep me at arms length, so it seemed. But things are changing. He laughed and laughed at the way the Lord had led me to go to a Jehovah's Witness, knock on his door (well, ring his bell), share my faith and give him a Christian magazine. John came to my 70th birthday party *and* brought me a nice present.

So from my original prayer, asking to be able to share my faith in the village, so much has opened up. And there is more, but the above is surely remarkable evidence of the fact that the living God inspires us, hears us, and answers us.

Otherwise, we have to say, "What an amazing coincidence... and another... and another..."

# Chapter 13

## The Greatest Miracle

It was September 2013, and I had been doing regular walks around the village since Spring 2011. They were proving rewarding as I met such a variety of interesting, engaging personalities. How do you see the people in *your* neighbourhood? I must confess that I had a rather two-dimensional view of most other folk in our village – until I actually met and conversed with them. They had been forms, shapes, silhouettes that drove past me in their cars, or walked their dog the other side of my garden hedge, and they were backs of heads watching televisions seen through windows as I, another shape or form, walked briskly past their homes on my way to the postbox.

But now they were coming alive, as the shape revealed depth and became a three-dimensional person, with character and personality, history and humour, family and interests, and talent and qualities. I found that all sorts of different people walked round our village – children taking the family dog for a walk, old men shuffling round on sticks, and mums and dads hurrying to meet their children from the local primary school. Others were weeding, planting and mowing in their front gardens, and always ready to pause and pass the time of day, whilst there were those who sat on the bench under the wrought iron mill, plough and Viking sailing vessel that comprise the village sign. (Viking sailing vessel? – our village was reputedly founded by a Viking, and the village name is a simple corruption of his name). Everyone had a story to tell, and so did I. But mainly I listened, and learnt people's names, and discovered that every occupation imaginable seemed represented within the six hundred or so souls living within our community. There are teachers, shop assistants, dental receptionists, bus drivers, shelf stackers, general managers, doctors, architects, refuse collectors, an archeologist and people engaged in innumerable businesses. And when one starts to consider the various leisure interests, the list again seems infinite. Great people, and some were born-again Christians, which made them my brothers and sisters in the family of God. But I wanted to share my faith with more people – not inflict it on anybody, but meet people who might ask me about it. And I prayed, and sometimes together with Wendy, that the Lord would give such opportunities (which he did) and that we might see people in the village get born-again into the family of God.

So I walked, and stopped, and chatted and listened. It was early afternoon and I had passed the village school where the playground was buzzing, as I walked by gardens in various stages of colour and tidyness. There was a bungalow a little further down the road on the right that had intrigued me when I first came to the village, as the garden was more jungle than wilderness. There had been three dirty cars rusting on the drive, and a sign on the gate read 'KEEP OUT. MAD DOG LOOSE'.

\* \* \*

'KEEP OUT. MAD DOG LOOSE'. Where was the sign these days? I had made up my mind some years earlier just *who* the mad dog sign referred to – but for the past few months, the sign had gone. In fact, it had been replaced some time earlier with a friendly sign reading HELP YOURSELF, or something like that, over a box of apples. Or was it cauliflowers? Certainly, something was going for free.

As I approached the bungalow, I noticed a lady leaning over the gate, cigarette in hand, and chatting to another lady who had presumably been passing. Could this be the owner of the mad dog and 3 rusting cars? But the lawn had been mown, the drive cleared of corroding junk, and the lady was smiling. Her companion called out "See ya" as I approached, and walked to the houses opposite.

"Wow – you must be new to the village," I called out. "Your garden looks great. It used to be a jungle."

"I've been here some months now darlin'. By the way, I'm Freya," said the lady with the twinkling eyes and broad smile. "And thanks for saying about the garden."

"I'm Barrie," I replied, and told her I had been in the village about thirty years, and that her bungalow had always had a jungle for a garden.

"You should see what the inside was like," she said. "We rent the property and we've had no hot water and no central heating since we got here. Have to boil water in a kettle. Actually, it's been really difficult ever since we moved in here. Anyway, what's *that* on your face?"

In fact, my right cheek was crimson. A pre-malignant lesion had appeared, and the doctor had given me some cytotoxic (cell killing) cream, which I applied every day. The right side of my face had gone yellow and crusty, and looked rather like an oatmeal biscuit stuck to my cheek. People's expressions were quite amazing as they looked at me, blinked, stared, and then (usually) asked me what had happened to my face.

"Been in a fight?" or "Heck – what happened?" or "You never were good looking, but that's horrible." And when I said it was a pre-malignant lesion, Christian friends would either take a step forward, lay their hand on me and pray, or take a step back and curse it – or just stare. And then it dropped off, and some said, "I did pray for it," and some said, "I did curse it" and the doctor said, "Good cream, that."

But it left me with a bright rosy cheek for a while, provoking Freya's question. I explained, and she told me to wait by the gate while she ran back indoors. She soon returned with what looked like a stick of rhubarb. "It's Aloe Vera," she said. "Keep rubbing it on your cheek. It will heal quickly."

Freya was clearly a very pleasant lady, and had shared various homes with a friend for twenty years. Just good friends – they really were, but nothing more. And three dogs, two ferrets and a few cats. My faith came up in conversation, and I later returned with a copy of my book, *THERE MUST BE MORE TO LIFE THAN THIS!* Well, she had given me Aloe Vera!

\* \* \*

It was towards the end of November and Wendy and I were planning a little party for early December, where we could spend some more time conversing with friends over a glass of wine. We sat down, and I made a list of some of the people I had met on my walks, and we arrived at a guest list of around sixty. I had only met Freya that one day in September, but thought she and her house partner should be included. Sixty might seem a lot of people to invite to one's home, but we have a fairly large house, we both enjoy entertaining, Wendy loves cooking, it was a buffet and not a sit-down meal, and perhaps a quarter would decline anyway as Christmas is such a busy time of year. As it happened, half declined as there was a village outing to a Christmas show that we did not know about.

It was Friday morning, and the local supermarket delivered the food, Wendy got busy in the kitchen, and soon sideboards were decked with plates of sausage rolls, dips, and a myriad of other delicacies. Shadowy figures appeared weaving their way through the illuminated stars, angels, Bambi, polar bear and various other electrical adornments that Wendy uses to try and delude me into believing I am living in Santa's Grotto every December. Then the shadows materialised into friendly faces on the doorstep. In no time the sitting room, hall, kitchen and dining room were humming with conversation, with the doorbell periodically playing its various tunes.

"Hello darlin'. Thanks for the invite." Freya and companion entered the dining room where around fifteen people were sipping and chatting.

"Now, I want to ask you a personal question darlin'," said Freya, and suddenly the room went very quiet.

"You can *ask*," I replied, giving my stock response to the question that is fired at one from different people at various times in life.

"Well, I've asked your wife and she says it's alright," said Freya, probably oblivious to thirty listening ears.

"Go ahead," I said.

You could hear a pin drop.

"Will you baptise me, but I'm not sure I've accepted Christ yet?"

Never, ever, had I been asked such a straightforward question about becoming a Christian, and I was not quite sure how to answer it. 'Here, kneel down in front of all these people and ask Jesus into your life' was a possibility that I quickly dismissed, and decided that –

"Why not come round one evening next week, and Wendy and I can discuss it with you?" seemed a more appropriate response.

"Whenever you like my darlin'," was her reply – and Monday was the mutually convenient evening.

And so the party continued.

* * *

Freya came round on the Monday evening, and shared some of her life story. We felt that she had made some sort of commitment to Jesus when she was young, but we prayed together about this, and Freya was obviously keen to come into a relationship with God. We suggested she might like to come to some of our church meetings, and also the fellowship meetings of our Full Gospel Businessmen's Fellowship, both of which are usually at our home.

Would we baptise her, and she had set her heart on the sea at a beach in the village of Waxham? The North Sea in December? In winter? I chickened out, though Freya was clearly up for it. So we decided on 8th June, the Sunday before her birthday.

Meanwhile, Freya was coming to our meetings, where we sang our hearts out and really looked to see God meet with us. She looked radiant, and prayed out loud in the gatherings. "I float home on air after the meetings, find myself singing the praise songs, and people keep asking me what's happened. So I tell them!" she said.

But it was not just praising and telling people. A lady who at that time was homeless came to one of our meetings. "Come and sleep at my place. No problem. No charge." A man who was going through an extremely difficult time involving homelessness started coming to our meetings. "I've got a room for you. Move in to my place. My house partner is there for conversation too. Do come." Love for people as well as God, and oozing with generosity whilst experiencing extreme difficulties herself, Freya was such an inspiring example to the rest of us. She was not perfect (are *you*?), and had much to learn (don't *you*?), but she was a radiant and inspiring member of our little church.

We had asked God for opportunities to witness, and we had been given them. We asked for people to get saved, born-again, converted or whatever term one uses – and Freya was now speaking about how she had come to know the Lord.

The day of the baptism approached, and rain was forecast. Then a number of our more regular members felt unable to come to the event, which disappointed Freya and left Wendy and me somewhat bewildered. But nearer the time, good things happened, and after I had printed some invitations to the baptism, Freya went round the village inviting people. She was so engaging with the people, and though it was the day of the village fête, about a dozen drove down to the beach around fifteen miles away to listen to her testimony, watch us praise God, film it on camcorders, take photographs and witness the baptism. Some of our irregular members came, which was a great encouragement, and despite the forecasters, the Lord blessed us with a hot sunny day so that we could also picnic on the beach.

Life is not easy for new believers, because although God is almighty and above all, there is a very real spirit world where other powers opposed to God are operating. It is a spiritual war that we do not fully understand, but about which we know enough to get victory. There were difficulties over her tenancy, and court proceedings. She needed to find somewhere else to live – but where? She was offered a new house in the village, and then was told that it was a mistake and she might get a house the following year in a village a significant distance away.

All this was not good for her health, and we prayed for strength and provision for her, while she somehow 'hung in there'. The cats kept breeding – three dogs, two ferrets and eighteen cats!

She prayed. We prayed. She had been housed in our Norfolk village, and was previously in Wales. Where would she be housed next? The eventual answer was a brand new house just two miles away, and the first Sunday after she moved, she arrived on our drive riding a bicycle.

\* \* \*

Jesus has always healed sick people and worked amazing miracles of guidance, protection and provision. But the greatest miracle is that of a changed life. Back in 1965, he changed my life forever. In 1972 he changed Wendy's life forever. In 2014 he changed Freya's life forever – and the change shines out for all to see.

We have a God who answers prayer, heals the sick, and who changes lives. And the greatest miracle? – a permanently changed life.

# Chapter 14

## Toothache

"You're a dentist – would you pray for my painful tooth please?"

\* \* \*

After qualifying as a dental surgeon at the London Hospital in 1968, I spent five very happy years working at a practice in the county of Dorset. Shaftesbury was a delightful hilltop town of Saxon origin, when it was called Palladwr, though the Romans changed the name to Shaston. On a clear day you could see as far as Glastonbury, forty miles away across the Blackmore Vale. It was in Shaftesbury that I first came to really *enjoy* dentistry, meeting a wide variety of interesting people day after day, and feeling I could help them. It was whilst at Shaftesbury that I married my University sweetheart, bought my first house, and welcomed our first two daughters into the family.

Whilst back at University, a friend had visited a church at South Chard in Somerset and been deeply impressed with what he had seen there. There was no preplanned 'service', except inasmuch as they met at 10.30 a.m. and 6.30 p.m. Sundays, and most weekday evenings. There had been just a handful of people who felt that the Lord had called them to meet in this way, and yet the Spirit of God was clearly leading not only their meetings but also their general development. As prayers were answered and miracles were experienced, their numbers grew and a small building was erected in the garden of the home where the meetings had started. Then an extension was added, and a number of people gave up their secular work to be in full-time ministry. No-one was paid a salary, but each expected the Lord to provide for them if he really wanted them to continue in ministry. The full-time workers, and others, visited various towns, cities and countries, preaching the gospel and healing the sick. A further extension was added to the building, then a gallery, and later a dormitory for weekend visitors as the work grew and numbers continued to increase.

After qualifying and settling in Shaftesbury in Dorset in 1969, I started going to the South Chard Fellowship quite regularly and found the presence of God almost tangible. Uncle Sid (quite a small man) and Auntie Millie (not very small) were the founders, and I had not met two people more full of praise and humility. Another couple, Trevor and Sue Lancashire, were pastors in the church, and were an inspiration to so many of us.

"Do you know the Barrys?" said one of the leaders of the church. "Nelson Barry and his wife Margaret. They used to come here, but now meet in their home in Trowbridge. It's near you, isn't it?"

I had to drive around forty miles to the Somerset church, and I could see on a map that Trowbridge in Wiltshire was around thirty miles away. So they were 'near us'. They met during the week on a Thursday evening, and a week or two later, I drove over to introduce myself and enjoy the presence of God in their home. Nelson was a tall handsome man, whose retiring manner was in contrast to Margaret's rather forthright nature. They had made a living dealing in antiques, and now in late middle-age, spent less time engaged in antiquities as they gave themselves to the Lord's work in their area.

I had noticed two Mercedes cars on their drive, and assumed that I was not the first to arrive for the meeting. But

I was, and so I enquired about the cars. "His and hers," said Margaret. Nelson smiled and explained. "Some people believe we have joined the prosperity cult," he said, "but it's nothing like that. The Mercedes are both secondhand, cost us no more than a new Ford, enable us to take quite a lot of people around, and never break down!"

I enjoyed the meetings there. We praised and worshipped, and there was prophecy, tongues, interpretation and other 'gifts of the Spirit' that were a normal part of the meetings of the churches we read about in the New Testament. Sometimes they would ask me if I 'had a word' and I would share whatever I felt the Lord had been teaching me at that time. I was grateful to Nelson and Margaret for encouraging me to speak and teach in those days.

They had a son called John, who was married with a baby. John and his wife were lovely believers, who seemed to really exude the glory of God. He was without work when I knew him then, and like his father, he was a man of few words. But I have found that such a demeanour is often accompanied by wisdom, and I listen attentively to such people.

We were in the kitchen at Trowbridge after a meeting, drinking coffee and consuming cake.

"You're a dentist. I've got toothache – would you pray for my tooth please?" asked John.

John was the first person to ask me to pray for a dental problem, which is one reason I clearly remember the occasion after more than forty years. Since then, there have been several cases of people coming to me at or after meetings, and asking me to pray for their teeth. "Is it OK for me to ask?" they sometimes add. "You being a dentist, I wasn't sure whether to ask." I reassure them that I will generally pray for *anybody* with *anything*, though I sometimes smile and say, "But if the Lord heals your tooth, please keep quiet about it. Could be bad for business, you see!" Just a joke, and always taken as such. If you *do* get healed, tell the world and give glory to God.

There was silence in the kitchen as I asked John what the problem was with his tooth.

"It hurts," he replied, "especially if I press on it, or bite with it."

It was a classic dental abscess, where the pulpal tissue (the 'nerve') within the tooth was dead and infected, with the pus escaping through the tiny hole in the root apex and infecting and inflaming the surrounding tissues. Press on the tooth, and you squeeze it into the swollen, inflamed gum, and "Ouch". An abscess can be extremely painful and on occasions, if left untreated, gives rise to septicaemia, a very serious condition.

"I've never prayed for a tooth before," I explained. "But the Bible does teach us that Jesus healed every sickness and disease that people brought to him, and that he is 'the same today'. Let's pray for that tooth."

I was not sure whether I should lay my hand on John's tooth (which would cause it to hurt) or his head, or where. I opted for his shoulder, and prayed, asking that the power of God might come upon him and bring healing to his upper left lateral incisor. Probably because I am a dentist, I can remember the tooth.

"How does that feel now?" I enquired, and John said that he felt it was somewhat better, but believed the Lord would heal it regardless of how it felt.

* * *

It was around three weeks later that I was next at the Trowbridge meeting, and John was there.

"How's the tooth?" I asked.

"No more trouble," John replied.

As a dentist I am aware that the infected material of a dental abscess can discharge, after which the pain and other symptoms abate. For a while. But there is usually a small lesion on the gum over the tooth, through which a slow discharge continues until the tooth is treated or extracted. So I looked at his gum, and could see no lesion. On subsequent occasions, when visiting the church in Trowbridge, or just calling in on Nelson and Margaret because they were friends, I would ask, "How's the tooth?" and the answer would be "Fine, thank you." And I never saw a lesion on the gum.

Both sceptics and cynics will understandably ask whether John saw a dentist, other than me, to confirm that his tooth was healed. They might ask if X-rays were taken. I think it highly unlikely that John went to a dentist after the pain went. There was pain, and we asked the Lord to heal it. After asking, the pain stopped. Why go to a dentist? Did people healed by Jesus in Bible times subsequently try to get proof they really were healed? If the Lord is an integral part of ones life, prayer is also integral, because we are talking about relationship. For those outside the kingdom and family of God, there has to be continual doubt and denial. For those of us who are members of the family however, these things are simply a part of everyday life. Our God hears the prayers of his children, and responds to them.

\* \* \*

Harry Greenwood was one of the full-time ministers in the church at South Chard, and he travelled widely, preaching, teaching, and praying for sick people. On more than one occasion he was asked to pray for a tooth with a cavity, and when he did so, the Lord filled it with gold! 'Come on!' I thought. 'Pull the other one' – and excuse the pun. But at that time there were other reports of teeth being filled with gold in response to prayer, especially but not exclusively, in South America. I do not accept everything I am told, but sat down and prayerfully considered what I was hearing. Why do teeth decay and develop cavities? Because we have refined carbohydrates in our diet. Sugar breaks down to form an acid, and attacks the protective enamel for twenty minutes every time it is eaten. When this has produced a hole in the enamel, bacteria penetrate and destroy the underlying dentine resulting in dental decay, and often pain. What is the best filling material? Gold has always been the best filling material in my opinion. Why? Because it will seal with the tooth around the margins (no leaking), and it is insoluble when attacked by the acid produced in the mouth by sugar. In Bible times there was no refined sugar, and the enamel on the teeth protected them. These days, the enamel does not withstand the attack following sugar ingestion. But gold does!

\* \* \*

I have two other endearing and enduring memories of the Barry family, one of which involves John. Once again, it was after a meeting, and we had congregated in the kitchen to drink coffee, eat cake, and enjoy fellowship. John was present as usual. To say he was a man of modest means would be an understatement, and if I had been asked at that time to give an example of someone who demonstrated true humility, John would have been high on my list. He had no work, but not for want of trying. He never complained. He always said how good the Lord was to him. He had no car, and either bicycled to the meetings by himself, or arrived with his wife pushing a pram. He had a radiance to him that I have often found over the years to be present with godly people.

"The Lord has told me to give you this," he said, and held out his hand. I reached forward, wondering what John might have for me. In fact, what on earth *could* John have for me, because the man had nothing of his own, it seemed.

A one pound note! This was around the year 1971 or shortly after, and one pound coins were not introduced until 1983. I did not want to take it. I had a car, and John had none. I had money in the bank (some, but not much) and John had none, I was sure. How could I take this one pound note?

But I did, and it was the most precious and most valuable one pound I have ever received. I placed it in my pocket, thanked John and gave him a hug. And there it remained for months, and perhaps years. It was in my blazer pocket, and I placed nothing else there. When I put my hand in my pocket, I felt the note and recalled John's generosity. In his poverty, John was generous, and he was obedient to God, and as such I believe he would have been rewarded.

There is no place in the kingdom of God for meanies, and there is no place for people who do not obey God. One pound in the early 1970s would be worth around thirteen pounds at the time of writing. In my relatively early days as a Christian, John was a striking example to me of humility, generosity and obedience, and I believe there is a lesson for others here too.

The second memory of the Barry family was quite a long time later, after I had been in Norfolk for several years and had lost touch with them.

"Have you heard? Nelson Barry has gone to be with the Lord." I had bumped into a mutual friend who was still in touch with the family and church in Trowbridge. "It was a great funeral, full of praise and testimony to the goodness of God. And after they had buried his body, Uncle Sid danced on the grave, like they were rejoicing in heaven and welcoming Nelson in." Uncle Sid, pastor of the church at South Chard, must have been well into his eighties at the time.

Dancing on the grave. Why not? I feel great joy in my heart at times, and express it by dancing. David did in Old Testament times, and Jesus has certainly been good to me. I doubt I will have a grave, as I will probably be cremated, though I am not too bothered about what happens to my body once it is dead. I will still be alive, and entering heaven, by the grace of God. But should you feel like dancing with the angels, please feel free. Rejoice!

# Chapter 15

# *I Leant Against a Lamp Post and Wept.*

"After thirty-two years of continuous pain, it had gone." Colin leant against a lamp post on that sunny October day, said 'thank you' and wept.

\* \* \*

Six feet and several inches tall with broad shoulders, Wayne stood out in a crowd. Well, he would, wearing those sports shorts in church and everywhere else. Wayne was super fit, and taught difficult boys at a difficult school. He thrived on the challenge, and was probably the best thing that had ever happened to the kids. If they threw a chair at him, he'd catch it and put it back. If at the end of a carpentry lesson the table was accidentally nailed to the floor, he would laugh with them.

Wayne had given his life to Jesus whilst working at a school in our area, and he was never quite the same again. A decent chap became a more decent chap. He and his family moved back to Birmingham for a while, but after a few years they returned to Norfolk where we enjoyed their company again.

Rugby was another of Wayne's passions, and a few years ago he started playing for a local club. Then he became their coach. After that, coach and player. A man of faith, but able to muck in with the rugby team too. Why not? – that's what Jesus might have done.

The church called *Liberty!* that meets in our home was having an outreach evening, 28th July 2013. The Methodists in the next village had very generously lent us their building for the meeting, and an evangelist we knew called Ash Kotecha was speaking and praying for the sick.

Wayne went forward for the laying on of hands and prayer, explaining that he had sustained a nerve injury, and that for some considerable time he had experienced the continual sensation of snakes slithering up and down his neck under the skin. Ash laid his hand on him and in Jesus name, commanded healing. Wayne looked up and said, "It's gone!" And not only was Wayne instantly healed, but he has stayed healed.

\* \* \*

A member of the Methodist church that had lent us its building had been seriously ill for many years. The problems had started in 1982, and Crohn's disease was diagnosed. There were tests, pills, and potions to try and resolve the bouts of severe pain. In 1997 Colin underwent surgery, with around one metre of his intestine being removed. After an initial improvement, there was further deterioration from 1999, and in 2002 additional problems suggested that the pancreas was by then involved. There were no more drugs or treatment that could cure the condition, and further serious surgery was considered, not least as the debilitating pain was almost preventing Colin from eating. So in February 2013, a further considerable length of intestine was removed, though this did not bring about any remission, and tests, pills and potions were becoming an integral part of his life. Also, with his ability to absorb nutrients and proteins in particular being seriously impaired, Colin now started experiencing extreme fatigue.

On 8th September 2013 we had a second outreach meeting with Ash Kotecha, again using the local Methodist church building. Colin had some responsibility there and showed us round the building with regard to light switches, fire exits and suchlike. I thought he would stay for the meeting, but he decided to spend the evening at home and left.

I opened the meeting, welcoming the forty or so people present, and Ash in particular, and moved into a time of praise with my guitar. I play rather badly, I think, but love praising God. I hardly noticed Colin coming back into the church – curiosity had gained the better of him.

And then Ash was speaking, pointing us to some of God's promises in the Bible, and telling us of healings and miracles he had witnessed. He invited any who were sick to come forward for prayer and the laying on of hands, and one or two sauntered to the front.

"May I say something?" Suddenly Wayne was out of his seat and striding to the front of the church. "I came to a meeting like this in July," he explained, "and I had nerve damage in my neck from playing rugby, with the sensation of snakes going up and down. Ash laid his hand on me and prayed, and Jesus healed me. I was healed immediately and have had no more trouble since."

People were now getting up from their seats and around fifteen stood at the front. Amongst them was Colin. I heard him outlining the problems to Ash, who then prayed for him in Jesus name, speaking Bible promises. What happened next was something I had not witnessed before. Colin started saying, "I'm hot. I'm so hot," and he was opening his shirt and flapping it in an attempt to cool down. This continued for several minutes. I will now quote from Colin's own account of the evening.

"*On 8th Sept I went to a healing service, in my own parish, led by Ash Kotecha. I went, worn down by the knowledge that the pain wasn't going to leave me, but get worse. Worn down by the knowledge that I was (not so merrily) trundling along a road towards having my 'food' fed straight into my veins. I stood at the front of the church, with a few others. At no time was I touched by any other person (I knew that the power of prayer had more than helped me through the dark days at the beginning of the year.) The longer I stood there focussing on spoken words of Scripture I'd heard many times before, I became hotter and hotter (internally). It was close to unbearable, and the pain was still there, still as intense. At the end of the evening, the heat had gone, but the pain hadn't.*

*A couple of weeks ago I was aware that the pain was much less, and the sharp stabbing attacks were not lasting as long. And this is how it has remained. Instead of a daily pain level of 7-9, it's usually a level of 3 or 4. It does still hurt to sit in meetings, as in sitting still for long periods. It still wakes me up when I inadvertently move onto the traumatised area of my abdomen. The level of fatigue is still the same. But, overall, I feel just as I did approx. 15 years ago. And if this is the general level the pain remains at, you'll hear no complaints from me. A month later, I was walking along a path and I realised for the first time in over 25 years I had no abdominal pain or discomfort whatsoever. Nothing. I tested it by stretching – still nothing. I leant against a lamp post on that sunny October day, said 'thank you' and wept. Just a shame that I couldn't share that moment with anyone."*

* * *

Of course, some might argue that it was simply a coincidence that Wayne was instantly healed when Ash prayed for him, and likewise Colin. Or some would argue that it was psychosomatic – mind over matter. But the truth is so obvious – unless you are running away from God with your eyes (and brain) tightly shut.

Quite simply, we have a God who answers prayer, and who heals the sick, like he has always done, and who works miracles, like he has always done, everyday signs and wonders for everyday people living their everyday lives. Praise him!

# Chapter 16

## Please – Not 666!

Then I woke up in the middle of the night, and just knew it was 666. Help Lord!

\* \* \*

I never really set out to write a book. It was all due to our friend Toby Lewis, or perhaps it was the lady who asked me to speak to the Women's Institute in the mid 1970s. But behind it all was the God who had changed my life so dramatically way back in October 1965. Toby Lewis and the lady from the Women's Institute both played a part and I shall always be grateful to them.

"Write a book Barrie. Write a book." Toby was sitting in my dental chair in the Norfolk market town that I had come to love whilst examining, scaling, filling, extracting, and replacing the teeth of its lovely inhabitants. Toby lived some distance to the south of my practice, and in fact completed an eighty mile round trip for every appointment. I think I must have been sharing some story from the dim and distant past that still caused me to smile when he first told me I should 'write a book'. Dear Toby – always encouraging, always complimenting, always inspiring.

But I never thought I would actually write a book, or that 666 would get under the radar and sneak onto its pages.

\* \* \*

So what is the significance of 666? 666 is the number of the Beast in the book of Revelation, chapter 13 and verse 18. The Beast? – Satan. But the number is a clue to a man who will represent Satan on earth – the Antichrist. And so the guessing game begins, and surprise, surprise – in the eyes of some spiritual pundits every Pope has been seen as the Antichrist, every American president has been seen as the Antichrist, every autocratic world leader has been seen as the Antichrist, every decent political leader with a following... With such a poor track record at identifying the Antichrist, I am amazed at the enthusiasm with which some Christians hurl themselves into the fray, and then proffer, "I'm not saying this is definite, of course, but I'm 99% sure that the Antichrist is..." However, I do not want to take too lightly the fact that a political leader will one day arise and deceive nations, plunging this world into a spiritual abyss from which few will be saved.

So, believe me, I veer away from any association with the number 666, though I do not want to be superstitious about it. There was in fact a time when 666 stood outside my home almost every Sunday. Back in the 1970s, we had a church meeting in our home. It grew rapidly until we were crammed together like sardines in a tin, and had to move out into a community centre. The local Methodist minister shared my surname, and on one occasion I preached in his church and he preached in ours. A trifle confusing for some. But his son had joined us several months earlier, and proudly sported 666 on his motor bike number plate. It just happened to be the number on the bike, and he let it ride, if you'll excuse the pun. And then there is John, a good friend of mine who excels at all things outrageous – fifty press-ups using one hand on the floor of pubs, bungee jumping off a crane in the centre of our local city, advertising himself as a squash coach on the sides of his builder's trucks, and having a personalised number plate plus the numerals

666. He says he shares my faith, and really is a thoroughly decent chap!

\* \* \*

It was back in the mid 1970s that a patient who was a member of the Women's Institute asked me if I would speak at their local branch. I duly went along, spoke about the anatomical make-up of teeth, the speed of the new 'fast drill' and the chemical composition of toothpaste. There was polite attention from most, and a little thinly disguised boredom from others, with muted applause at the conclusion. But I could not help noticing that the one thing that caused everyone to look up, and most to laugh, was the fact that the main cause of losing false teeth was vomiting them accidentally down the toilet.

The next time I was asked to speak to a Sunny Corner Fellowship, or some group with a name like that, I made sure I mentioned that 'teeth went down the toilet' and also included the story of the married couple who shared a set of false teeth, and the man who vomited his out of the window from the top deck of a bus passing through the crowded streets of central Norwich. Obviously, this was what people wanted to hear, and having ditched all information on the speed of drills and composition of toothpaste, and incorporated more stories of people losing their false teeth at sea, of a retired general biting me and of the night I caught a burglar at the practice, I found that invitations to speak started coming in thick and fast. There was also a change in the nature of the gatherings; ladies' luncheon clubs were well-attended by well-heeled ladies, and Conservative Party evening bun fights had wonderful menus. This started to seem like fun, until I was asked to return, and realised I only had one talk. So having spoken at most of the luncheon clubs and dinner societies in the area, I found I was back on the shelf, with the exception of the occasional Women's Institute. At the time of writing I am again taking up speaking at secular occasions

(I just *have* to mention about being born-again though!), and have expanded my repertoire to five talks – *Looking Down in the Mouth*, *Licensed to Drill (Dentist on the Loose)*, *Patients From Heaven – and Other Places*, and two others.

\* \* \*

I retired in 2007, but continued to meet up with Toby. In fact, Wendy and I would meet up with Prof. Toby Lewis every six months for lunch together, and he would lean across the table and say, "Write a book, Barrie."

So I put a folder on my computer and named it *BOOK*. After that, when he enquired whether I had yet started, I could truthfully say that the start of a book was on my computer.

And the day came when I felt inclined to 'have a go', and so I listed the stories from my after-dinner speaking of years past, and thought I might write a short chapter on each. Until... I looked down my list concerning the fate of dentures, and how the retired general bit me, and a few dozen similar happenings, and I realised that these were trifling matters when compared with the way the God of the Bible had virtually invaded my life at the age of twenty-one, changing Barrie the atheist into Barrie the born-again Christian. I considered how he had healed me of Irritable Bowel Syndrome, guided me in making decisions at crucial times in my life, provided for me as I went through several difficult years financially, and so on. I became excited and made a new list, and started writing. Three weeks later, I had written my first book! I had to go through it many times, correcting typos, rephrasing, editing generally, and asking Wendy and various literate friends to read through it and make suggestions. I was especially encouraged by a friend of around forty years, who at times had been something of a spiritual father to me, the evangelist Don Double.

I approached a traditional Christian publisher, who emailed back with words to the effect 'who are you, and who will read you?' My thoughts entirely, I conceded, and decided to shelve the project. But two weeks later, Don Double's encouraging words caused me to go back to the same publishers, who asked me for a synopsis of what I had written, and thirty minutes later for the whole book. One week later they offered me a contract.

The book was proof read, the cover designed, and eventually it was sent to the printers. Wendy and I joined two other couples that we sometimes holidayed with, and set off for the Atacama desert to do some exploring and hiking. After around ten days of gazing at sand dunes and craggy rocky wilderness, we drove over the Andes into Argentina, and ended up on an estancia, a ranch where we relaxed, strolling around the grounds watching a variety of interesting birds, and seeing a llama being untangled from its tethers (Wendy helped with this, and was seriously drooled on by the animal), while our companions rode off on some of the estancia's horses. There was no Internet (well, there was a system of sorts, but it did not work for us), and an intermittent mobile signal.

* * *

I woke up. It was night, and I felt quite disturbed. What was it? Suddenly I knew. Despite checking through my manuscript dozens of times, and although others had done the same, I had entered a Bible reference incorrectly. I crept out of bed and found my iPad, and was soon running through the manuscript. 666 – it should have read 663.

The words that Jesus spoke were 'spirit and life', we read in John 6:63. So why had I written John 6:66. It was a verse that I was really familiar with, so I had not looked up the reference. No doubt my proof readers assumed I had looked up the reference and got it right. But I *knew* it – no need to look it up. And yet I had put it down wrong. 666.

To so many people this would be such a minor problem, but I do not like mistakes. Any mistakes. In addition to the fact that the reference was wrong, I really felt that the devil had somehow slipped this in. It's *his* number, and I knew it was his number, and if I had to have a mistake in the book, I certainly did not want it to be 666 in any form.

I prayed that somehow it could be changed, as the number of copies being printed was well into four figures, and I had given my final OK over the Internet from the airport at São Paulo, after finishing my very final proof-read on the flight. And that had been at least ten days earlier.

I was up early, but the UK was well into day. I used my mobile as this was the only means of reaching the publisher. No signal. I walked round the grounds and tried again. No signal. I continued walking, and found that on one side of the property I had a signal of two bars. My publisher was surprised to hear me.

"I thought you were somewhere up the Amazon," he said with a laugh. "What can I do for you?"

I explained, but he said it was too late. The text had been sent to the printers over a week previously. They would be well into it by now. They might have finished.

But I had put the wrong reference, I explained, and my publisher reassured me that "nobody ever looks up the references in books anyway." "I do," I interjected. "Then you are the exception," was his reply.

"But it says 666, and I feel the devil is making a joke of it," I pleaded.

The publisher said he would telephone the printers and see how far they had got, but it was too late by now to change anything. I prayed.

Five minutes later a text arrived. I cannot remember the actual words, but I can certainly remember what it told me. Something like, *Surprise, surprise. Printers were just about to start when I phoned them. 6:66 changed to 6:63. Printing now in progress*

\* \* \*

Answered prayer for everyday people in everyday life. I had made a mistake – everyday people do. I felt guilty and embarrassed by it – everyday people do. But my Father in heaven loves me, and carried out what the publisher had explained was probably impossible.

Never limit the Holy One of Israel, for nothing is impossible to our God. He simply loves people like me – and people like *you*!

# Chapter 17

## *Thumbs Up!*

Whilst praying for Walter, he wept and shook uncontrollably, continually giving me the thumbs up!

\* \* \*

It was around nine months ago, at the time of writing, that a young middle-aged man from a nearby village asked me if I would consider calling in to see his father. "It's been a really difficult time," said Mark. "Dad hadn't been feeling well for quite a while, and the hospital gave him all sorts of tests. They have told him he's got motor neurone disease, and he can't walk now, and even talking is difficult. What has really concerned me though, is that when the hospital asked him his religion, he wrote down 'Atheist'. It looks like he's dying, and he has no faith, and I think he is angry and blaming God. Would you consider coming to visit him sometime?"

I had actually met Walter a few years previously when I had picked up Mark and taken him to a meeting. Mark is a plasterer and gardener and... well, he can turn his hand to many things. He is also a very faithful member of our local Full Gospel Businessmen's Fellowship.

I was not sure whether I should really call round to see Walter, as he was obviously not too favourably disposed towards God at that time, and I felt that that feeling might be extended to God's people as well. Back at home, I prayed about visiting Walter, and Wendy and I did so in our prayer time together several mornings. After a week or two, I felt I would wait for a convenient evening, and go and knock on his door.

Around ten days later, I drove over to Walter's home, and rang the bell. "Remember me?" I asked Walter's wife Flo, as she answered the door. "I'm Mark's friend. I met you one evening when I picked him up for a meeting."

"Cors I remember you," Flo smiled. "Come on in. Walter will be pleased to see you."

It was a homely place and I immediately felt comfortable. "Hello Walter," I said to the rather thin man sitting in an armchair just inside the door. He tried to greet me, but was unable to speak with any clarity.

"He's asking how you are," said Flo, as I sat on the sofa where the waggy-tailed dog came and laid his head on my lap. "I'm fine Walter. Sorry to hear you've not been so good recently," I replied.

Would I like a cup of tea? Was I keeping well? Don't mind the dog! Such small talk made me feel at home, and I spoke briefly of our six daughters living in five different countries, the busyness of retirement, and of how much their son was appreciated in our Full Gospel Fellowship.

It was time to leave, as short visits to sick people are usually appreciated more than lengthy ones, unless it is immediate family. Walter was unable to stand up as I extended my arm to shake hands with him on my way out – but something unexpected happened. I knew that Walter was a professing atheist, and suspected it might be because he was angry at being so ill. Maybe. I had decided that I would not ask Walter if I could pray with him, but nor had I decided not to. I would see how I felt the Spirit of God moved me. As we shook hands, I heard myself saying, "It's been good to be with you today Walter, and may the power of God come upon you and bring some healing to your body."

I had not intended to pray for him, but as I did so, he wept and shook uncontrollably, and kept giving me the thumbs up sign.

I waited two or three minutes while he composed himself, and there was a twinkle in his eye and the hint of a smile as I bade Goodbye to his wife, asking if I might call in again sometime. Thumbs up was Walter's answer.

Around two weeks later I called round one evening, sat on the sofa with the dog, chatted for around fifteen minutes, and got up to go. Should I pray for him again? I shook his hand, felt no particular leading to say anything other than "I'll come and see you again sometime, if that's OK." The response? – thumbs up and much nodding. So back at our home, Wendy and I continued to pray regularly for Walter, that he would be healed.

A fortnight after this I drove round to the small village where Walter lived, and rang the doorbell once again. I was greeted by Walter's wife and the friendly dog, and shown through to the sitting room where Walter smiled and attempted to say Hello. The three of us conversed as best we could, and after around twenty minutes, I felt I should see where Walter was with regard to 'God' and related matters.

"Walter, before I go, would you like me to pray for you?" I asked. He smiled, nodded and gave me the thumbs up. I walked over to him and laid my hand on his shoulder, and again asked that the power of God might come upon him and bring healing to his body, as well as for joy and strength for him and his wife. Again Walter shook violently and wept, all the while giving me a vigorous thumbs up sign. And they both said Amen.

I saw Mark some days later and told him what had happened, and he used the word 'miracle' to describe his father saying (well, thumbs up) that he would like prayer. But Walter was now going to have a PEG (Percutaneous Endoscopic Gastrostomy feeding tube) fitted, so he could be fed by-passing the mouth. He was not allowed visitors for a month. Wendy and I continued to pray for him from our home.

\* \* \*

It must have been six weeks later that I next visited, and Walter was looking significantly better. He was still unable to speak clearly, but appeared to have put some weight on. His wife was feeling encouraged, as Walter was now able to walk again, aided by a frame as he set out round the village. The doctor had talked about him driving his car again.

We talked about the weather, the local football team, and the improvement in his health. Maybe it was the PEG or maybe it was the power of God coming upon him. But all healing comes ultimately from our Creator, so I thanked my Heavenly Father.

"Walter," I said. "When I pray to God, I am actually praying to my Father, and I would like you to know God as your Father too, especially when you pray to him. But that means giving your life to Jesus, and trusting in him. Would you like to know God as your Father?" I proceeded to briefly and simply explain the gospel, and when I asked if he would like me to lead him in a prayer giving his life to Jesus, there was a vigorous thumbs up. I explained that as he could not say 'Amen', a thumbs up sign would be his way of making my prayer his prayer. And so I prayed with Walter, and when I finished, I put my thumb up, and he put his up alongside mine. And he wept, shaking violently as ever. It was a very moving time. We then thanked God for Walter's greatly improved health, and asked for more healing. Thumbs up.

About two weeks later, a lady in our church had a birthday party, and as Mark was her gardener, he was present. We chatted for a while, and then circulated, until around an hour later, Mark came over to me, clearly concerned. He had received a call on his mobile phone, informing him that his father had suddenly deteriorated, and an ambulance was going to the house for him. Mark and I prayed together, and then he left in order to be with his parents. And two days later, Walter died.

I was quite shocked, as I had not expected it, and was really disappointed, because I thought he would improve still further. It was very sad, as we had become friends and I knew he was loved by his family.

Wendy and I went to the funeral in their local church, and it was packed. What a popular man he must have been within that community. But although he was loved by his family and community, he was loved even more by the God who had become his Heavenly Father only two weeks or so before. And now he was with his Father.

Why did he get so much better? He was nearly eighty – but why did he die? We will probably never know the answers to these questions, but I will always thank God for the dramatic improvement in Walter's health over the few weeks I prayed for him, whether it was the NHS or God or both. And I praise God for that healing, for while in no way meaning to detract from the value of the medical profession, all healing comes from God. I look forward to meeting up with Walter again one day, because in a very real way, he had crossed over the line from death to life a couple of weeks before he died.

/

# Chapter 18

## Angelic Protection?

Seriously, Rachel and Chris, my daughter and son in law, could easily have been killed. How they escaped is inexplicable, except for God's intervention.

\* \* \*

"DRIVE ON THE RIGHT. DRIVE ON THE RIGHT!" shouts Wendy as I emerge from Rachel's drive in Ploeren in Brittany, and set off down the left-hand side of the road. Oops! Swerve!

I don't really have too much of a problem remembering to drive on the right-hand side of the road, except first thing in the morning. In fact, we have been going to France for years, and nearly always drive there. When the children were quite young, but old enough to travel, we needed to decide where to go on holiday, and considered certain factors. Firstly, my wife liked speaking French, and secondly, I enjoyed drinking wine. Easy – cross the channel and indulge in both.

My very first trip to France had been at the age of around seventeen, when we were staying as a family in Brighton. We had not been abroad before as a family, and my father decided he would take us to France for a day. So we drove along to Folkestone, parked the car and caught the ferry as foot passengers to Dieppe. I can remember very little about the day except that my sister and parents bought souvenirs, and I could not find one thing that appealed to me as such.

Eventually I made up my mind, found a barber, and came home with a French haircut. I'm not sure anyone noticed, but I was proud of it. And I didn't go abroad again until I was married with a family of my own, and by that time I had a wife who liked speaking French, and I was developing a passion for red wine.

We were not wealthy enough to stay in hotels in those days, but opted for a campsite where tents were already erected. They were great days, and the children and I have lovely memories. "Dad, see how far you can get the cork!" chirped a young daughter as we returned from town with a bottle or two of sparkling wine. I would aim far and high, and the girls would scamper off after it. "Dad, see if you can hit that cow!" was a later development, when we were camped next to an orchard where cows grazed. I missed! Not all our activities involved sparkling wine, but another game I played was firing out the cork, replacing it loosely and gently shaking the bottle to make it jump out again – but not too high. My daughter Sarah was fascinated with this, and one day while my back was turned, decided to have a go herself. I would have told her *not* to push it down too hard, and I would have told her *not* to shake the bottle with all her might – and I would have foreseen that the cork would have *exploded* from the bottle and left sparkling wine dripping from the ceiling, the overhead light, the curtains, the furniture, me, Sarah.... and I believe my wife had something to say about it too!

But I drove on the right-hand side of the road. However, it is a little difficult to remember to do this all the time, especially when you have reached three score years and ten, and it's early in the morning.

Which brings me to my daughter and son-in-law driving through Dorset recently. I had celebrated one of those 'big birthdays', and five out of six daughters, plus grandchildren, cousins and in-laws had joined Wendy and me for dinner at our favourite hotel. My daughter Rachel and her husband Chris decided to have a romantic weekend away in Dorset, on their way back to France, where they have lived for around seven or eight years now. Originally it was work that took them out there (Chris designs marine navigation instruments on the southern coast of Brittany), but since becoming part of a French-speaking church, that has determined their place of residence even when the chance to return to England has presented itself. In fact, they have seen the hand of God in their original move there, and seek his will in a very earnest manner in all things.

They were returning from a rather charming guesthouse and heading east towards the ferry terminal in Portsmouth, when the one in the passenger seat (I'm not saying which) shouted, "You're on the wrong side." They swerved back onto the left side of the road.

"Wow – that was amazing," said Rachel. "We've been driving for a while now – and on the wrong side of the road all the time."

"Thank God that we did not meet another car," said Chris. "The Lord really is looking after us."

And then, a few minutes later, they slowed down and looked at each other, saying, "But we *did* meet another car. It was a few minutes ago, and it passed us on the wrong side!"

They should have been killed, or at least seriously injured. Driving along on the wrong side of the road, and meeting a vehicle coming the other way. Was the other car *also* driving on the wrong side? It must have been. Was there divine, or angelic, intervention? We will never know, but I too thank God for the amazing way the other car was also driving on the wrong side of the road.

I thank God for protecting my family, because I love them all dearly. And I thank God for the innumerable times he has protected me, often while I am totally unaware of it. I wonder about *you*?

Of course, this is not a case of answered prayer, like "We're driving on the wrong side of the road. Lord, please protect us." But I do pray regularly that the Lord will be with each of my daughters and their respective families, leading them, providing for them, and *protecting* them.

There are those who would say, "What a coincidence that another car was driving towards them, but also on the wrong side of the road." And again we are back to the zillion to one chance. Quite simply – it was a miracle!

# Chapter 19

## Hotline to Heaven!

"Hang on to your telephone tight, dear – and listen," said Bob, and then proceeded to pray for the lady.

* * *

We grow! Once I was little, and now I am big. Too big – I need to diet! But our growth is not just physical, but mental, emotional, spiritual, and in so many other areas of life. I can remember timidly giving my first injection at Dental School, but I grew better at it with time and experience. We grow in our relationship with the Lord and his people, the family of God. Well, most do, though sadly there will always be those who drop out, if my understanding of the parable of the sower is correct, and we each need to ensure it is not *us*. There will also be those who cease to join with, or identify with, the family of God – perhaps they never really understood what they were signing up to when they first made a commitment to Christ. But in all these areas of life, and more, people grow.

I love the way members of the family of God really care for each other. I recall an occasion when, having started a new dental practice and being snowed under with work, I was unable to get to the shops to buy meat for the evening meal. My receptionist must have mentioned it to a patient, who immediately jumped up and said, "What do you want? I'll get it." And she did, though I hardly knew her. She was a born-again Christian, and it showed. I got to know her and her husband later. They were not well off financially, and one winter's day arrived home to find a large amount of coal had been delivered. They really needed it, and could not afford it, but someone else had arranged it and paid for it. It thrills me to see people in the church we are part of helping one another in all sorts of practical ways. I love this family of God, and feel deeply saddened at the way some people just drop out.

We grow in our prayer life. Most non-Christians I know seem to think that prayer is mainly 'asking God for things'. When I first became a Christian, I used to ask God for things quite a lot. Well, I was a hard-up student ("Please help me make my grant last out the term.") and had exams to pass ("Please help me get a good result."). Prayer for others became a significant part of praying as time passed, and praise and worship, enjoying God's presence, and listening are all major parts of my praying these days. We grow.

We also become bolder in our praying. When a fellow Christian told me of a need, I would say that I would pray about it – and did. As I grew in prayer, upon hearing of a need, I would say, "Let's pray about this, *now*." And we would pray on the spot.

Over the past twenty or so years, praying over the telephone has become a fairly regular occurrence. In fact, I probably pray with people over the telephone several times a week, and occasionally several times a day.

It must have been around twenty years ago when two of my daughters, separately, would phone me from time to time and ask me to pray about a problem or situation that was troubling them. Why not? The Lord is with us wherever we are, and is not limited to one place. He is with both of us on the telephone, or these days with Skype we can have conference calls involving several people, though I have yet to pray over Skype.

"Please Dad, I've got a problem with CAD. Can we pray?" It was Rachel, my second daughter, who had studied Industrial Design at Loughborough University and was now working for one of our leading companies designing, manufacturing and selling kitchen appliances.

"What's CAD?" I asked.

"Computer Assisted Design. I am trying to get a handle on a jug, but there's something wrong. Or I'm doing something wrong with it. It just doesn't work," she explained.

So we prayed. And guess what – a few days later the design came together properly. Our God is alive, he hears, and he responds.

With regard to our local Full Gospel Businessmen's fellowship, we often need wisdom. Who should we get to speak? Or, the speaker cancels – what shall we do? Quite often I will pray with another of the leaders over the telephone. Recently we have needed a new treasurer, and there seemed absolutely no-one to do it. We prayed, and a few days later I received an email from a member asking if he might be considered. And he has proved so good at it. Thank you Lord! Also recently, the Fellowship's finances have caused me some concern. Over the telephone, two of us prayed about it. At the time of writing, that was six weeks ago, and this week we received an email from a Christian in a far part of the world asking for our bank details, because he feels he should be supporting us. I have never met the man. Bless him, and thank you to our God who is with us when we pray – over the telephone!

We have a good friend called Bob Waters, a godly man, elderly (like myself), and a widower of several years. He is a Field Officer with the FGB and leads worship at many meetings and conferences. A visiting speaker told Bob he would like to pray with him, and ask the Lord to provide a partner for him. "Amen to that," said Bob after they had prayed.

Some time later, Bob was giving a concert at the village hall in the Norfolk village of Blofield. He also gave words of testimony and offered to pray for anybody with a need. A week or so after that, he received a phone call from a lady whose sister had been at Bob's concert, enquiring whether he could pray for her. "How do I get you to pray for *me*?" the lady asked.

"Hang on to your telephone tight, dear – and listen," said Bob, and then proceeded to pray for the lady.

Another week passed, and Bob felt he would like to follow up the telephone prayer, so he phoned the lady and arranged to meet her for a cup of tea. They got on well, and met again, and again.

"If she's the one you've got for me, Lord," prayed Bob before driving Connie to the Suffolk seaside town of Southwold, "Then could you provide two parking places next to each other on the quayside today."

As they reached Southwold, they saw that a circus had arrived and parking places were in short supply. But there was one place – and as they approached it, the car next to the space pulled out, making two. They parked in one, and another car drew in alongside. Bob jumped out and handed the surprised driver of the car his camera, explaining what he wanted him to do. Bob proceeded to open the passenger door, and as Connie came out, went on one knee and proposed marriage.

"Of course I'll marry you, Bob," said Connie, smiling broadly, as the camera clicked. The wife of the driver-cum-photographer ran round the car to see what was happening, and burst into tears. At the time of writing, the wedding takes place in a fortnight.

What a God we have! What a Heavenly Father, who hears us when we pray, meets needs, provides wives, and responds to his people when they get together on the telephone!

# Chapter 20

# *Balkan Rhapsody*

"Don't put the phone down Dad. I'm in love!"

\* \* \*

My four daughters are musicians. Well, such terms can be somewhat relative, and if you heard me strumming my guitar, you might say, "Barrie is *not* a musician." Let's just say that they play a lot better than I do. My daughter Naomi graduated from Nottingham University with a degree in music, and felt the Lord was calling her to work for him in the Balkans. Her awareness of this call came in a strange way. She knew about the conflict following the break-up of the former Yugoslavia in 1991, when the political unrest throughout the area resulted in civil war breaking out in the various states of the nation. Coverage of the conflict in Bosnia was on our television screens daily, but it was only after the war had ended that Naomi realised that God was calling her to work there. It came about like this.

*Whilst in my last year of study I was unsure of what the logical next step would be. With a music degree it wasn't clear to me where I should be going next. What was important to me however was that my time at University had brought me to a place where I wanted to serve God with my whole life and wanted to devote it to Him in whichever way He asked. My preference was 'radical' and preferably with plenty of miracles and drama, but I realized that a quiet, stable life lived in humility alongside the lives of others could also be used for God's glory.*

*After a time of prayer one evening I went to bed and as I closed my eyes saw what looked like images on a T.V. screen. In fact two images came to the screen; the first was of many, many people walking diagonally across my 'screen'. They walked obviously together in one stream looking tired and weary. It appeared to be a long journey with people of all ages, and quite some baggage. The second image was of chaos and confusion; of people hurrying and seeking and looking for a place to go, not knowing which direction to take and allowing panic to steer their course. They were not long, complicated images, but they seemed immediately significant. So much so that I asked the Lord, "What is this? What is this about?" I felt strongly that the reply was 'Bosnia' and that I was being asked to pray for this land, which had previously barely awoken my interest. As I started to pray, I experienced an overwhelming sense of compassion. Tears flowed and this feeling that God urgently wanted to reach out to these people began to take a place in my heart.* (Naomi's own words)

Shortly after this Naomi received a visit from a good friend of hers called Adele, and told her that she was intending to go to Bosnia. On returning home, Adele came across an advert entitled 'Go, Go, Go – Do You Want to Go to Bosnia?' – or similar – in a Christian youth magazine. It was a recruitment advertisement by a small mission called *Novimost*.

After an interview at the mission's headquarters, Naomi was provisionally accepted. No-one working with the mission was paid by them; if the Lord had really called them, then they needed to ask him to provide for them. In the meantime, they suggested she find work to save a little money before setting out.

It was a joy to have Naomi living close to us for a while, as she worked in our local city in a tea-shop – and a nightclub! After just a few months, the time had come for her to depart, and within a week or two of handing in her notice, she was living and working in Mostar.

\* \* \*

I will never forget my visits to Mostar, and also another city in the region, to which Naomi felt called. The historic bridge called the Stari Most (old bridge) over the river Neretva had been destroyed during the war, and everyone could remember where they were and what they were doing when they heard about its fall. So we crossed the river on a temporary bridge, though later a splendid replica of the original was erected. Whatever the people of the three different ethnicities felt about each other, they were so warm and gracious to Naomi's visitors. Well, they certainly were to me, and I enjoyed wonderful times of feasting at parties with the Romany people, and attempting Albanian dancing to a ghetto blaster. Naomi was a popular person within the various communities in the city, and was an integral part of the worship group in the Evangelical Church of East Mostar.

I would love to read a book of Naomi's adventures in the region, and I could catalogue a few from memories of my own times out there with her – but she would be embarrassed. However, the time came when she felt she needed to be sure that working in the region was still God's call on her life, and she 'took a year out' and played viola with the Sarajevo Philharmonic Orchestra. One of my great regrets in life is that I did not get out to the Balkans to hear her play, but I did watch recordings of Naomi on television, where the orchestra was featured very regularly.

\* \* \*

It was the autumn of 2003 when Wendy and I visited Naomi. We had been married a few months, and flew out to Dubrovnik where she would meet us the following day. I had told Wendy about the brilliant sunshine and blue skies there, and we arrived late afternoon and enjoyed a walk in the warmth of the evening sun. That night there was an electric storm, and the rain pelted down throughout the following day. Naomi arrived with her friend Claire, and one of the first things they did was bale out the car. It had been broken into some time previously, and their Romany friends had bent the forced door back into shape, though the door seal was the wrong size and did not fit as well as it should have. It leaked!

Naomi drove to Mostar first, but the windscreen wipers were not working. This meant that periodically, she had to lean out of the window and clear the screen manually. But that was Bosnia – different, fun, and a great place for those looking for a challenge in life.

After Mostar we continued to Sarajevo, where Naomi had moved into a room in a family home. It is a fine city, and we enjoyed exploring it with her, and sampling the wares in some of the cafés and restaurants. She was just embarking on her sabbatical year when she would be playing with the orchestra.

And then our time was over and Naomi was driving us back along the scenic road to Mostar, twisting its way between high mountains, whilst looking out across valleys on both sides. And on to Dubrovnik, where we enjoyed a blue sky and late summer sun as we gazed out from the walkway high atop the city walls, listening to the toll of the bell echoing dolefully across the sea of terracotta rooftops. An open-air restaurant. A live concert in the main square. A call on my mobile – daughter Rachel had just given birth to their first child, and we had another grandson. The reception was not good. His name? 'Roger!' *Roger?* We listened to the message again. 'Elisha'. *Elisha!* Welcome, grandson Elisha. And so to our hotel, and the following morning we returned to the UK.

\* \* \*

Emails! What an amazing way of communicating – instantly or at one's leisure, lengthily or briefly, and for free! When Naomi was not home, or we were not in Bosnia, we corresponded regularly by email. And by telephone. But so often, it was emails. One incident that we followed through emails will always be with me.

I have a good friend called Don Double. He is an evangelist, and when time permitted, I would be part of his temporary team at tent crusades that he used to hold in villages and small towns. Before each campaign started, he would pray that the greatest villain in the community would come to the crusade and be so soundly converted that everybody would know that God is real. Every community has a greatest villain.

One day I, along with others who prayed for Naomi, received an email from her. Apparently, a man known to be a villain had threatened to come to a worship meeting she attended, where he said he intended to shoot people. The meetings took place in a community where a number of Moslem Roma (gypsy) people had given their lives to Christ. The man was big – probably over 30 stone (420 pounds) in weight – and had a gun. He was known as one of the greatest villains in the area, and Naomi understandably asked us to pray.

The man did indeed go to one of the worship meetings, where he pulled out his gun and started waving it around. The leader of the meeting, himself a converted Moslem, spoke to the intruder about the love of Jesus, and before the evening was over, they were on their knees – and a one-time villain had become a child of God. I received another email, this time suggesting praise rather than prayer.

Shortly after the incident, the man was baptised in the local river, which was a stunning witness to those who knew about his previous life.

A month or two later, I was in Bosnia visiting Naomi, and one evening we went to the worship meeting in that community. The man was not there, but he was not far away.

When we came out of the building to drive back to Naomi's flat, we found that her car had been vandalised and was not drivable. It was almost pitch dark, but we became aware of a huge rugged man approaching. Seeing our plight he put his shoulder to the vehicle and pushed it into a shed where it would be safe for the night, while we were given a lift back to Naomi's home.

Prayer – a crutch to lean on, or a cry to a living God who can do absolutely anything? Such as protect vulnerable people from a gunman, and change a villain into a child of God. And in all these things, Jesus is glorified, because that is what it is all about.

\* \* \*

It was January 2005, and Wendy and I were again heading out to the Balkans. This time our primary destination was Nis in Serbia, where Naomi was joining us. Her year in Sarajevo had come to an end, and she had returned to Mostar where she was as busy as ever working with the people there.

Why Nis? It's quite a long story, and this visit was to be the first of several. Vlada and Sonja were part of the leadership team of a church in the city, and some years earlier had spent time training and working at the church we were part of in Norfolk. Now they invited us out to see them, and to speak at their church, and as Naomi was fluent in the language I called Serbo-Croat (also know as Serbian or Croatian or Bosnian, each with its own distinctive dialect and emphases) we decided it would be useful and fun if she joined us. We flew to Budapest, and then on to Sarajevo, where we met up with Naomi. The city was enshrouded in snow, and we walked, skidded and slid along to a hotel. The next day we flew on to Belgrade, where Vlada was waiting for us. For two hours he accelerated, skidded, braked and skidded again along the roads to Nis. Nis (pronounced Neesh) is a beautiful city with a fine and heroic yet brutal history. Empires had marched through this city on several occasions. We stayed in a flat over a dental surgery, which itself was a revelation to me. Several copies of Playboy magazine adorned the waiting room's magazine table, and I was intrigued with the practice generally. "Ceegarette?" asked the dentist as we sat in his surgery, waiting for his next patient. "No thanks," I said – so he and his wife lit up and exhaled smoke across the sterile worktops and drill units. He showed me exquisite models of work he had carried out; their implants and bridges were of a high standard.

"Raki?" he asked, offering me a glass of the local firewater. I declined, and he and his fellow-dentist wife knocked back a generous shot each. Their patients would arrive soon.

Was I impressed with his work? Yes I was. Did I carry out implants? No I did not. Perhaps I would like to refer some of my patients out to their surgery in Nis? I would of course bear this in mind.

A large slab was produced from a drawer containing clinical instruments. It was broken into sizeable chunks.

"Chocolate?" he offered with a smile. "No thanks. I'm a dentist," I was tempted to say. But "No thanks," showed a little more grace.

Vlada took us on a walk up a mountain. It was snowing a minor blizzard with the wind against us, and our host was gracious – he hates the snow! "Have you come far enough yet?" Yes, we had, for although we love walking in the snow, we too can be gracious.

Vlada took us to a restaurant, and for once we did not have the ubiquitous 'meat and beer'. Was this their staple diet? No – meat, beer and *bread* was the fayre served at most meals. And at this restaurant we had meat, bread and *potato*. Hooray – something different. And then from the restaurant to the home of a church leader for meat, beer, bread and more potato. Delicious (truly) – but we thought we were going to be really ill. So much food.

We trudged through snow. We spoke at meetings of the church, with Naomi and Sonja as interpreters. They loved Naomi, with her warmth, humour and personality.

We bussed back to Belgrade, and explored the fort overlooking the Danube, where a dog took a shine to us and followed us for a couple of hours or so. We lunched at a classy hotel in the centre of the city, but the waiter forgot the chips, ran out to McDonald's and returned with a good portion for each of us. Then a flight to Sarajevo, and the most beautiful bus ride along that same mountainous road, but with the magic of snow. Snow was covering the mountains, encrusted on the trees, layered on the rooftops, and giving an overall Christmas card atmosphere wherever we looked.

Mostar. I loved that city and its people – but Naomi loved it more. We stayed at her flat before returning to Sarajevo, to fly to Budapest, to fly to London. It was late that evening. We talked about life, about the Balkans, about the Lord – about meat, beer and bread! Then Naomi sat down and spoke to us of her desire to be married one day. It was an emotional subject. She would like to be married with a family – or to have real peace in her heart that the single life was God's will, and would be fulfilling. The Lord had made it very clear to her that she was to be working for him there. She hoped to get married and have a family some day, and yet, though the men she met in the Balkans were fine people, she had not yet sensed the necessary degree of compatibility required in a marriage. Wendy and I felt deeply for her in this, and after praying with her, promised to continue praying together every day until she either met the right man, or felt peace in her heart that marriage was not for her.

We returned to our home in the UK and every morning without fail, we sat together and asked the Lord to bring the right man to Naomi or give her peace that she was to be single. We wondered how long we would have to pray!

* * *

One evening, just three months later, I was on the telephone to Naomi. It was quite late, and I asked what she had been doing that day. She told me that what she was *about to do* was to make a chicken salad and put a movie on. I pointed out that as it had just gone 10 o'clock in England, it must be after 11 o'clock in Bosnia, and I would put the phone down and let her get on.

"Don't put the phone down Dad. I'm in love!" Naomi spoke quickly, probably fearful that I would put the phone down before she had finished.

"In love? With whom?" I exclaimed.

"Well, you have been praying, haven't you?" she said.

I admitted that we had prayed faithfully every day since we had last been with her, and she told me how she was playing Dora (the name of her viola – rather like some people give their car a name) in the worship group on a recent Sunday morning, when a young man had walked into the church. This man was not 'local'.

Herman had arrived in Mostar from a University in Amsterdam where he was completing his degree in Cultural Anthropology with a dissertation on reconciliation between different ethnic groups in the evangelical church of East Mostar. Initially there was not a romance, but meeting at friends' homes, getting to know one another... and the rest is history.

\* \* \*

Romance was in the air, love blossomed, and they were married in Mostar in May 2006. It was a tremendous time, with the sun beating down on the cavalcade of cars hooting their way through the city. Michael Palin was filming a new television series in Mostar, and my son-in-law Tim happened to spot him the next day. He marched up to the great celebrity saying, "Hi Michael, I'm Tim. How's it going?" and was told that the previous day his crew had had to abandon their filming on the iconic Stari Most bridge. He said that there was so much hooting "from some wedding."

Naomi and Herman lived and worked together in Mostar for a few years, and later returned to Amsterdam where they now live with their four little girls. I have read that no father feels that any man really matches up to the husband his daughter deserves. I think I must be an exception to that rule, and love each of my sons-in-law, believing they are almost as near to the 'perfect son-in-law' as one can get. But should I ever have doubts about Herman, I will remind myself that after years without a husband, Wendy and I prayed, and within a matter of a very few months, the Lord brought along Herman and presented him to Naomi as *his* choice for her husband.

I love thinking back to this example of answered pray, as I feel it demonstrates the Fatherheart of God in such a loving, intimate and romantic way.

# Chapter 21

## Pennies From Heaven

My accountant sat behind his desk, perusing my annual accounts. "There seems to be an unknown factor again," said Bill. "Whenever you really need money, someone turns on a huge invisible tap, and cash just pours out for you."

"I'm so glad you've noticed that," I replied, at which Bill uttered a groan and said, "Oh no. I'm not going down that route!"

\* \* \*

I'm sure it's true that love of money is the root of all kinds of evil, but money itself is not evil – money is *necessary.*

Without money, we would not pay our mortgages, buy groceries, have clothes, or be able to enjoy most of the bare necessities of life. But *love* of money… that's different.

There is a wealth (please forgive the pun) of teaching in the Bible about money. We are told to *work* for it (not always popular), to be honest, and to be generous. Most of all, we are told to put the Lord first when it comes to finance, which too is not always a popular teaching amongst some Christians; however, we are encouraged, both in the Old Testament and the New Testament, to give responsibly to the Lord *before* spending money on ourselves or other things. There are promises that we will be looked after, but always within the overall context of giving the Lord priority in our finances, as well as the rest of our lives.

To summarise what we find in the Bible – put God first in your finances in practical ways; be generous; trust God to look after you.

The application of the above can result in one's finances being a real adventure, and I would like to share with you something of my own journey in this area. I have known abundance and scarcity, but also experienced challenges whilst learning to trust. At times it's been a joy, at other times it's been tense, and generally it's been, as I've said, an adventure.

\* \* \*

Dentistry is a profession in which one can make a lot of money! I have known a few dentists who have gone bankrupt, usually through alcohol or simply spending far more than they have been earning, and occasionally by attempting to provide the very best dentistry whilst working under the National Health Service. But for every dentist that goes bankrupt, there are so many more who enjoy boats, fast cars, large houses, and a generally affluent life-style. I personally knew one dentist who had other businesses, a Rolls Royce and an aeroplane, and there are many others who have prospered in like manner.

But although material wealth seems to offer so much, it never really delivers. We each look for fulfilment in life, and money beckons and seemingly promises to unlock the door to this elusive contentment. Yet the more we have, the more we want. I have been privy to many cases of dentists chasing after financial wealth in such a manner that they have crossed the boundaries, cheated their patients and the NHS, and ended up disgraced. I could add 'impoverished', but this is rarely the case, as they always seem to bounce back, and again chase that elusive goal for all they are worth.

At the age of seventy, my home is a little larger than the average, my car is a little older than most, my holidays are a little more exotic than those of my friends, and I am a very contented and fulfilled man. But it has not always been this way. Let me tell you about it.

* * *

I would like to give you a brief over-view of finance in my life, and you will see, firstly, why I am so grateful to God for being such a good Father to me and, secondly, why I have come to trust him over the years.

My parents were not always well off. My mother came from quite an affluent family, and met my father, a bank clerk, whilst working together in Cambridge. His family were of more modest means, and my parents struggled at times financially. When I was quite young, my father had a serious nervous breakdown after catching fire when his car went up in flames, and some years later, he suffered a further breakdown. On both occasions, he was unable to work for significant periods of time, but we nearly always had a car, and did not go short of anything much. Most of my childhood memories are happy ones.

As a teenager I decided that I wanted to be a dentist. I wasn't sure this was possible, as none of our family had even been to University. No-one. Ever. I was not really aware that dentists were well paid – I just wanted to be the man in the white coat, bringing pain-free dentistry to people's lives as opposed to some of the traumas that I myself had experienced.

I passed my respective 'O' and 'A' level GCEs, was given a place at the London Hospital to study dentistry, and a grant of £8 a week to live on. I made ends meet, just about, but couldn't help feeling a little envious of the rich boys, with their fast cars, fast women, snappy dress and posh accents.

During my five years at dental school, colleagues would sometimes speak of what they were really looking forward to in life. Often, cars were involved. "I want a Mini Cooper S," said one, oblivious to the fact that this jargon went right over my head. A mini is a mini is a mini... isn't it! "I want a Marcos when I qualify," said Rob. I would not have recognised a Marcos if I had tripped over one – but apparently he got it.

Me? I wanted to qualify, work in the High Street looking after families, get married, have a boy and a girl (just like my parents), see them get married, settle down in comfort, produce grandchildren for my wife and I to dote on, and grow old with dignity. Money? I never really thought about it, but assumed that all would be well.

And then at the age of twenty-one, I had an encounter with Jesus. I changed. My life changed. Everything changed, including my hopes and dreams. My future? I wanted to know God's will for my life, enter it, enjoy it... maybe working in the High Street looking after families, getting married, having children... Money? It was tight and getting tighter, but I started giving ten shillings a week to a missionary society, and financed it by foregoing lunch in the students canteen and sometimes having a boiled egg in my room instead. All *was* well.

But there was a multitude of surprises awaiting me.

Having qualified, I drove down to Dorset in an old banger of a car to work at a practice that I felt the Lord had directed me to. Many of those who had trained with me seemed to be raking in a fortune already, but I earned £7 in my first week as a dental surgeon, though after a year or so it increased to around £80. I could have found much more lucrative work elsewhere, but I married and we were happy renting a small home furnished partly with secondhand furniture. Neither my wife nor I felt we *needed* more money.

In 1973 we felt the Lord was telling us to move to Norwich, and buy a certain rundown practice in the city. There was a problem – none of the companies that usually backed dentists would touch the practice. They referred to it as a 'dead duck' and told *me* not to touch it either. But surely God had directed us there.

My father had not enjoyed much promotion in the bank, but a past colleague of his was now a manager. My father looked him up, took him out to lunch, bought him a couple of beers – and I went into his office and asked for a loan. My tongue is slightly in my cheek as I write that, but he did offer me a loan, which needed to be repaid in ten years. I asked for twenty-five years, but he was adamant – ten. My wife and I asked the Lord to send me patients, as my predecessor at the practice had seen eight patients (maximum) a day for four days (maximum) a week, taking home £2,000 a year before tax. (Did he need to pay tax on that?)

What happened? The Lord sent me around *forty* patients a day (minimum) five days a week (minimum) and my practice loan was repaid to the bank in ten months. Not ten years, but ten months! That is the God I seek to serve – he's my Father, you see.

With a growing family (three little girls) and being increasingly busy with God's work in the city and county, we bought our first ever *new* car – a Volvo estate, with a little bench seat facing out the back window for the girls.

Patients kept flooding in, and so I added a second surgery, third surgery, fourth surgery and fifth surgery during my first nine years there. And each surgery had a dentist or hygienist working in it. When the work of the church increased, which usually meant helping people or speaking in places, I worked less days a week – either three or four.

And then the unthinkable happened, and my wife and I separated, and later divorced. To this day we each have a different perspective on what exactly happened, though I have never denied that I got myself into a dreadful and inexcusable muddle. My 'sin' was apparently unforgivable (on earth) though the Lord was gracious and merciful and made it clear it *was* forgivable (in heaven). But this awful episode left me (and no doubt, my wife also) with difficult emotions to handle. For me, there was the guilt of my part in the break-up of the marriage, the rejection of feeling unforgiveable, the frustration of spending months seeking reconciliation, with total lack of success, and the grief of being separated from my family, whilst realising *their* grief at being separated from me.

How does one handle such a situation? And what are the financial implications? Throughout, regardless of how I *felt*, I spent time with my Heavenly Father, reading his word and worshipping. Secondly, I *had* to come to a place of forgiving myself and forgiving others involved. Without elaborating on this subject, suffice it to say that Jesus alone is the real answer. Also at this time, a couple I knew a little came to me and said the Lord had told them to invite me to live with them and their family for as long as I liked. I was with them for over six months, and they were a tremendous strength and support.

But there were serious financial implications. I agreed to give my wife our family home and almost half my income, before tax, which left me with well under half the amount that I had enjoyed before – and nowhere to live. I was told I was too generous (and received little thanks for it), but I really do have a Father in heaven who looks after me – and in style! I found a small, but beautiful, cottage, which I bought with a 100% mortgage! And the following year the Lord increased my income by 50% bringing me just about back to where I was before whilst enabling me to continue giving my wife her agreed amount.

Around this time I started a small branch practice in the town where the couple who had opened their home to me lived. My overall financial situation was precarious, and my accountant said I had a 50% chance of going bankrupt by opening a new surgery. The new practice thrived, as patients streamed in through the front door. In less than a year, I was adding a second surgery and taking on a new (Christian) dentist.

Just after this, I felt I heard God speak to me, silently but with exceptional clarity, telling me to open a Christian book-shop. Separated from my wife, and heading into divorce, this seemed like madness – but after asking several mature Christians to pray about it and tell me if I was wrong, they said they were quite clear that this was a call of God.

Well, try telling the bank manager that! He agreed with the 'madness' theory, and gave the project a resounding ' No'. But his local head office reversed his decision, and gave me a loan.

Well, try telling your accountant that! He told me I was committing financial suicide, and despaired of me. But Sonshine Christian Bookshop was born in November 1984, and continued for nearly twenty years. We sold hundreds of thousands of pounds worth of Bibles and Christian material, and people entering the shop often found healing, encouragement, resolution of problems, etc. etc. as the staff listened, spoke and prayed with them. I lost well over £100,000 in the process, but so what? The Lord had called me to open the shop, he provided for me throughout, and blessed me and so many others through it.

During these twenty years or so, the Lord enabled me to support my estranged wife and four children, my new wife (I remarried), and to keep the bookshop afloat. The main practice was sold in 1988, and I lived very slightly clear of an overdraft most of the time. My car was over thirteen years old when I eventually sold it, but it was a wonderful motor and served my children and me splendidly. I was more than well looked after.

I will mention one or two other financial aspects of life at that time. The bookshop was staffed by quite a number of people. Some were full-time paid, some part-time paid, and some volunteers. Many were friends (not always a good idea). At a time when the shop was struggling financially, a full-time member of staff was made redundant. It was by mutual agreement, and because of some things that had been said, I was surprised at having to give the person several thousand pounds. But I gave the money, and prayed the Lord would bless all of us. There was no enduring hardship, and the shop continued.

I asked a part-time member of staff if we could adjust his hours, whilst giving him the same number of hours and the same pay. He was a very kind man, and generous with his time. However, after a week or so, he told me he had seen a solicitor, that this was 'constructive dismissal' and that I should give him a significant sum of money (I forget how much, but certainly hundreds of pounds). I have never understood what it was all about, but I gave him the money he asked for, and prayed the Lord would bless him. I never saw him again, and the shop continued.

My second wife became ill. She had suffered emotional and depressive problems for many years, but it became much worse. Suddenly she was gone, seeking divorce so she could go to Canada and be with a man she had met on the Internet. I was barely on my feet after nearly twenty years of supporting my first wife and children – and my second wife wanted half of everything we had. I sold my dental practice and sent the proceeds in their entirety to her. I started work for the new young owners, on an income reduced by one third. At the age of fifty-seven, I increased the mortgage on my home by £100,000 and sent that to her in its entirety, together with three of my pensions. I retained the house, which was precious to both my children and me, and continued paying the increased mortgage on my significantly reduced income. Throughout this very painful time (I loved my wife), the Lord was so close, and to this day has met every need. Truly, life is good.

I had taken out a policy to cover a family member who felt financially vulnerable. They never needed it, and eventually the policy matured. I thought it had just ceased, and was amazed when the company told me that there was now a cash sum of £70,000. This was at a time when such help was more than appreciated. Well, until the surprise of finding that the sum legally belonged to the person I had set up the policy to help. They too were surprised, and said the money was 'morally' mine (their words) and they wanted me to have it.

No problem. Thank you very much. And then they changed their mind, and told me over the phone they had decided to split it with me, and keep 50% themself. No problem. Thank you very much for 50%. A week later they phoned again and said they had taken financial advice and would be keeping 100% of the sum. So I thanked my Heavenly Father that he always looks after me, and asked him to bless the person who now had the money.

On 1st March 2002 I took Wendy to a restaurant. I did not really know her, though we had been members of the same church for years. Her husband had left her eighteen years before, since when she had worked all the hours she could in order to bring up her two daughters. She had had just one holiday in eighteen years. We married on 1st March 2003. Wendy had no money, and I had a little – *and* a huge mortgage at age 58. It was early days for us, and I received an enormous tax bill relating to the years just before I had sold the practice, and its sale. I had virtually nothing with which to pay it, but – Wendy's house sold, and after paying off her mortgage, she had... I expect you've guessed... exactly the amount I needed for the taxman. "Don't borrow it from me. Just have it," said Wendy with the widest of smiles. Wow – what a wife. I can never fully express my gratitude to God for Wendy. The bill was paid, and less than a year later I managed to raise the money to repay her. She was so reluctant to accept it, but as she had never ever had any savings before, this was an absolute priority for me. And we had both seen the hand of God so clearly in all this.

* * *

It's a strange thing, but I think my accountant expressed the workings of my finances so well all those years ago. Remember what he said?

"There seems to be an unknown factor," said Bill. "Whenever you really need money, someone turns on a huge invisible tap, and cash just pours out for you."

But I have worked hard, always sought to be honest towards all, and mindful of those who were less privileged. In all aspects of life, I have tried to put the Lord first. Clearly I have failed at times, but we have a God who forgives and restores. Two of the unhappiest types of people I have met in this life are those who have sinned and not repented, and those who have been sinned against and not forgiven. If you fall, thank God for his grace and mercy, and get up and walk again with him. If others fall, forgive from your heart and show it with your words and actions.

So at the age of seventy, and still with a six-figure mortgage, I can honestly tell you that there are few people more contented, more blessed and more fulfilled than me as I sit here, tapping out this testimony of his grace, in order to encourage you.

# PART TWO

So, following a selection of answers to prayer and other acts of God where there has been healing, provision, direction and suchlike, both the mundane and the amazing, the underwhelming and the overwhelming, the everyday and the occasional 'special', be encouraged to step out and pray for people and situations yourself. If, like us, you are an ordinary person, be inspired – and do it! We read in scripture that God does not call many wealthy, sophisticated, or worldly-wise people, but uses people like you and me, – and he specializes in miracles. So I have written a few short chapters in Part Two on things that Wendy and I have found helpful – well, *essential* really – in getting heard in heaven and seeing answers on earth.

May the Lord bless you richly in your walk with him, and may you too experience the miracles God grants in response to the prayers of his children.

# Chapter 22

## One of the Family

Frank knew he should never walk between a parked truck and a wall, but he hardly gave it a second thought, when... the vehicle rolled back crushing him. He knew he was going to die.

\* \* \*

Within a family situation, children's requests to their dad tend to get strong preference over those of outsiders. Not that outsiders never get a hearing. I hope that people coming to me with requests find a listening ear, and when I can help, I like to do so. I think our Heavenly Father is like that, because we read that he sends the rain and makes the sun shine 'on the righteous and the unrighteous'. However, that does not mean that I acquiesce to *every* request that comes my way, either from my children or from others. Once again, our Heavenly Father is our example, and he certainly does not grant every request made; and sometimes we have to wait until the time is right. Father always knows best.

But my children have priority on my time and my resources. Why? Simply because they *are* my children. And this principle is clearly demonstrated throughout Scripture. The Jewish people were favoured above all others in the Old Testament, because they were God's children, though this also meant they came under his discipline. Consider the exile to Babylon for seventy years. But they had many requests granted and were a favoured people.

God is gracious and there are many times when he grants requests from people who are outside his family. Take Frank (not his real name) for example. He and his wife came to my home for supper one evening, probably the best part of twenty-five years ago, and he told me about something that had happened some years earlier. He was not interested in God – he was concerned about himself, Frank, and getting on at work and having a good time. God? He had heard mention, but usually in blasphemous expletives. He worked for a growing local double-glazing company. One day he was walking across the yard. He knew he should never walk between a parked truck and a wall, but he hardly gave it a second thought, when... the vehicle rolled back crushing him. Frank said he knew he was going to die, and in that instant looked up into the sky and shouted loudly, "God, help me." And when Frank shouted that, it was a desperate cry for help and *not* an expletive.

"And it just stopped," said Frank, gazing at me intently across our sitting room. "The truck stopped, and people came and moved it and got me out. So I know He's there."

Frank was not a practising Christian either before or after that event. However, through that incident with the truck he had come to realise that there is Someone 'out there', and Someone far more powerful than us. But after saying that, Frank would place a big full-stop there. Frank was not a child of God.

\* \* \*

God created people, and he did so in order that we might enjoy a family relationship with him. But man went his own way (sin), which got him kicked out of the Garden of Eden (separation from God). The sin was now in his DNA and was passed on from parent to child, with all mankind being separated from God by sin. No longer children, but strangers. So Jesus came and paid the penalty for our sin. For those sincerely coming to him, sin was now cancelled out. No separation, but family. No longer strangers, but children.

I grew up believing in God, because when I was a child I was told 'there was a God'. But I didn't know him. Later I decided there was no God, and became an atheist. I still did not know him, understandably. Then I met people who said they knew him. Nutcases, I thought, though they did seem to be decent people. Why did they say such things – about *knowing* God? I investigated, argued, remonstrated, mocked, fought... and one day, sensed the presence of God. Around one month later, I surrendered my life to him. He changed me, and I've been different ever since.

I was born in September 1944. I was born into a family and my life began. In October 1965 I was born again into a new family – God's family – and started a new life. Now I was one of his children. Now I could pray to my Heavenly Father.

But in the New Testament, there is a little more to entering the family properly. The person entering would ask the church to baptise them, as an indication that God's family recognised that their old life was now over, gone, dead and buried with Christ.

Also in the New Testament, the person entering the family of God would ask the Lord to baptise them. This second baptism was not with water, but with the Holy Spirit, and was a sign that heaven recognised their new life, and empowered them to live it.

\* \* \*

I was rather slow about being 'born again', because so many people in churches told me it was not necessary. Some said it was extreme. But I found that Jesus said it *was* necessary (John 3:3). The people who said they were born again seemed decent people, and really sincere. And it was *Jesus* who said it. Scary stuff! So I got born again and became a child of God – *his* way.

I had been sprinkled as an infant, and my parents were told that that was baptism, and that I was now baptised. Later they told me that. Then I came to believe, and was challenged by the teaching of Jesus and the New Testament generally, with regard to being baptised now that I believed. There was pressure not to – but I felt constrained to be baptised. It was 1969 when I was immersed by a church in Somerset, UK.

Believers in the New Testament, in Jerusalem, later in Samaria, others in Caesarea, others in Ephesus... received the baptism of the Holy Spirit. Some people told me they had received this too. The Bible taught that we all should. This too was scary stuff. And they often spoke with new tongues. Help! But then, why should we be scared of something that God has for his children, and which does them good? Why? Weird! So I asked, and he baptised me with the Spirit. I felt the presence of God in quite a dramatic way, not just upon me but also as though permeating every cell of my being. Once more, I was never the same again.

So now I was born into his family, with the church agreeing that they witnessed I was a child of God (water baptism) and the Lord witnessing to it and empowering me through the baptism with the Holy Spirit. It was good to be a child of God. Hey – it was time to pray. Let's see what God will do.

But how should I pray? Well, it is all about relationship really.

\* \* \*

*'Unless one is born again, he cannot see the kingdom of God.'* John 3:3 '

*Now we are children of God.'*
1 John 3:2

# Chapter 23

## Get a Relationship!

**Think Outside the Box – and the Textbooks!**

"They had the stewards grab them, tie their hands and feet together, and lower them through the opening into the holding tent, while they led the others to Christ." A rather unusual way of handling people coming forward at an evangelistic campaign, but...

\* \* \*

Tom was part of the church where we were members. He came regularly for a year or so, and was much appreciated for his knowledge of scripture and ability to teach it. Life was not easy for him (or for so many others who came to the fellowship) and after a while he left and started going to another church a little closer to his home. But Tom did come and see us from time to time – when he had a bill to pay. They were, however, the only times when he came to see us. Initially, we would give him the money for the bill, but after a time or two, only contributed towards the total amount, and then one time he came and we gave him a cup of coffee but no money. We did not see him again after that. Wendy and I might be forgiven for thinking he only came round to see us when he thought we would help him pay a bill.

\* \* \*

Some time later, a man called Robin started coming to the church, and he too had very little in the way of resources. However, he continued coming regularly, though his pattern of life took him away for short periods of time. There were times when it was quite clear that Robin had no money, and yet he rarely mentioned it. Nor did he speak of the particular needs he had on a fairly frequent basis. Wendy and I and one or two others felt much more inclined to make small contributions to help see Robin through that difficult time in life.

\* \* \*

Wendy and I, and others we know, like to help people in the small ways that we can, but there is only one who can meets needs without limit. Our God is alive, and he can change people, change situations, heal sicknesses, and meet *any* need – financial, relationship, employment – *ANY!*

But in approaching him, we can be a 'Tom' or a 'Robin'. Do you tend to turn up at the throne of grace when you have a need, or are you to be found there often regardless of your situation? Please do not think that I am saying that if you only pray when you have a need, then that petition will be refused. Consider Frank in the last chapter, who had hardly ever prayed before. Nor am I suggesting that if you regularly spend time in prayer that you will be rewarded with petitions granted whenever you ask. Prayer can be very simple, but the overall subject is much more complex. At the end of the day, God is God and he will do as he pleases, albeit within the parameters of the revelation he has given us in scripture. In Deuteronomy 29:29 he tells us that there are some things that will remain a mystery, and we can waste precious time in trying to fathom the unfathomable.

Our God is not a type of heavenly slot machine where you feed in the 'right prayer' in order to receive the answer you desire. Some speak of prayer as though there is a correct formula, which if not met, will be thrown out by our loving Heavenly Father. Is that your understanding of our God? All prayers must have the suffix 'in the Name of the Lord Jesus', and in casting out demons, they *must* be sent 'to the pit', and cancers must be *cursed*, and you must never lay your hand on a person who is demonised... These statements and 'techniques' beg the question, 'Just what is our Heavenly Father like?'

Whilst in Bosnia around the turn of the century, I felt quite challenged by a lady I met who had been part of a two-lady evangelistic ministry based in South Africa. Now surely that must raise a few eyebrows even before we go any further! One lady had been prominent by appearing on television in a 'soap' each week, and the other was also a celebrity within that nation. They each had a life-transforming experience of Jesus, following which they independently sensed the call of God on their lives to 'go into all the world and preach the gospel.' They met up, conversed together on what they felt was their calling, and became a 'team'. This was all new to them, and I found the account of the lady I met interesting. They did not do it the textbook way, but just waited on God. They had not been taught 'the right way to do it', but simply threw themselves on the Lord, brought their needs and questions to him, and then launched out in what they believed to be the direction he was giving them. They prayed – and felt they should go and preach in Argentina. So off they went. I am not sure whether they had an interpreter, or whether they spoke Spanish, and I have no idea which part of Argentina they went to. It was the method that I found so refreshing. They preached, and called for the unsaved to come forward for salvation. Then they prayed for them, but if any of those coming forward became significantly agitated, they assumed they were demon possessed. They had erected a tent, and had an opening constructed in it several feet above the ground. When people appeared unduly agitated, they had the stewards grab them, tie their hands and feet together, and lower them through the opening into the holding tent, whilst they led the others to Christ. They then gave an appeal for the sick to be healed, and again, those who were agitated were tied hand and foot and secured in the holding tent whilst the sick were prayed for. After the ministry for salvation and healing was over, the stewards carried in those who had been bound, literally, and the two ladies cast out the demons. "And they came out, and the people were whole again," said the lady with a wide smile.

My point here is that these ladies may have broken all the rules in the book, but in throwing themselves onto God and spending time with the Lord, seeking his guidance and direction, they were keeping the most important rule – spend time with your Heavenly Father and do what he says. OK, that's dangerous, but to move out in ministry *is* dangerous. Know the Bible, read it and read it and read it and read it, and be familiar with what the Lord teaches us – then launch out! The result was that lots of people gave their lives to Jesus, many were healed of sickness and disease, and demons came flying out of the possessed.

* * *

Spend time with the Lord. Spend time with him often. Spend significant quality-time with him periodically. Let Jesus be your example and model in this – *he* certainly had lots of answered prayer!

Spend time reading his word the Bible – read it and read it and be familiar with it. Know the principles of prayer, and learn about who your Heavenly Father is, and what pleases him.

Most of all, just be *serious* about him. If a husband is serious about loving his wife, he spends time with her – and a wife with her husband. They *listen* to one another. We love him because he first loved us (1 John 4:19). Be real!

* * *

Wendy and I went to the national leaders conference of the movement that our little Norfolk church had joined. It was just over twenty years ago, and Wendy and I hardly knew each other and were not 'a couple', nor ever expected to be – but we just happened to be at the same conference. Neither of us were significant leaders in the movement, but we each had a small group meeting in our respective homes, and being at the conference gave us time to chat informally with those in leadership at a higher level.

Rules, law, conduct, procedures, etc. were being discussed over breakfast one morning. After a while, I cleared my throat and suggested, "I like to think that I can love God with all my heart, and do as I please." This was a little different from the general drift of the conversation up to that point.

"Isn't that rather dangerous?" said one of our elders, a man for whom I had a lot of time and respect as he was always friendly and never pretentious.

"It *is* dangerous," I replied. "But aren't we called to live dangerously?"

At this point, please do not hear what I am not saying, or read what I am not writing. If a person rarely spends time alone with the Lord, and does not read and read their Bible, it is indeed dangerous if they 'do as they please.' But if they truly love the God of the Bible, spend time with him, *and really know what he teaches us in his word*, then 'doing as they please' will see them living and serving within the parameters laid down by our God. True freedom *and* true holiness, in a real relationship with God.

## Little and Often

Charles Spurgeon, when asked, "How long do you pray for?" is reputed to have answered, "Twenty minutes – but *every* twenty minutes."

That may or may not be true, but I like the principle – keep praying. Think back to my friends Tom and Robin (not their real names, incidentally), where Tom can be likened to the person who prays only when there is a need, and Robin portrays the person who is continually aware of the presence of God with them, and speaks to him regularly.

My day is usually filled with prayer. I normally thank the Lord for sleep when I awake in the morning. Before we get up, and with our first coffee of the day by the bed, Wendy and I spend time reading a chapter of the Bible together, after which we pray. I don't know how many times I pray during the day, as I have never set out to count them. When something good happens – I thank God and praise him. When something bad happens, usually to other people who telephone or email us about it, I stop and pray for them. Often, when bad news arrives, Wendy and I sit down, or stand and hold hands, and straightway pray together about the situation. If a Christian telephones with bad news, I usually pray with them over the telephone immediately. Little and often – in principle, this was my practice whilst still working, though it fitted into a somewhat different pro- gramme at that time.

When you see a sunset, do you not want to leap in the air and shout praise to God, or maybe gaze with a sense of awe? At the time of writing, Wendy and I have just returned from a trip to the Arctic tundra of Hudson Bay in Northern Canada. It was November, and the sunrises over the snow-covered wasteland that stretched seemingly endlessly into far horizons, were incredibly beautiful, with, at times, deep crimsons hovering low in the sky, accompanied by pastel shades of pinks and purples covering so much of the eastern horizon. Some would gaze at it and say "Beautiful" or "Amazing," whilst others silently (or not so silently) say "Thank you Lord" or "Praise you Jesus!"

Brother Lawrence (no relation) in the 17th century 'practised the presence of God'. He had an awareness of the presence of God with him, and lived his life accordingly. He was real about God.

Answered prayer is not a reward for praying often, or much, or very regularly. We cannot 'earn' or merit the presence of God with us. All the Lord's blessings are truly of grace, which means they are undeserved – but that grace tends to flow through relationship. So, develop and deepen your relationship with the Lord, throughout the day, regularly, little and often.

## Help!

Crisis! It happens to you and it happens to me. It happened to Nehemiah... It happened to the psalmist... It certainly happened to Jesus. But what is your reaction? – it can reveal a lot.

Nehemiah probably assumed that all was going well with the reconstruction work back in Jerusalem. He, of course, was hundreds of miles away in Babylon, and around 500 BC, news took a long time to travel. When news came, it was that the work had ceased, the gates which had been burnt down were still unrepaired, and the people were dejected and in disgrace. His reaction? – he sat down, wept and *prayed*. (Neh.1:5). When the king asked what was wrong, he *prayed* before responding, and God gave him favour with the king, who permitted him to return to Jerusalem to oversee the work of rebuilding. Were these prayers he had memorised, or had written down so that he could read? Of course not – they flowed from his heart. This was a man who had a close relationship with the Lord, and who was used to conversing with him. He knew his God.

The psalms were written by a number of people, with David composing many of them. "Help!" is a recurring cry to God. Psalm 12 starts with "Help!" So often today, there is a cry that sounds like a prayer to God, but is really just a blasphemous explative. "Just words," say those who one day will stand before their Creator and give an account of their lives.

The psalmist's cry, in fact, flows from his relationship with God. You may recall the story of Frank at the start of the previous chapter. Now, that was probably an expletive he had used in the past, but on the occasion described there, it was *prayer*. Desperate prayer, but *not* a cursing shout. Likewise the psalmist – "Help Lord!" was a prayer. And we read of many places where that prayer was answered. We have just mentioned Nehemiah, and the psalmist adds his own testimony, "I sought the Lord, and he heard me, and delivered me from all my fears." (Psalm 34:4)

We are encouraged to have an ongoing relationship with the Lord, and we are fools if we neglect it. There are so many accounts in the Bible, in history, and from contemporary people that our God hears cries for help, and answers. This is not to discount doctors, medicine, the emergency services, counsel from the wise and suchlike, but there is only one who can do absolutely *anything*. Whatever else you do in times of emergency, cry to the one who loves you *and* is all-powerful.

## To Be Like Jesus, Be Like Jesus!

If we want to be like Jesus in ministry, healing the sick, seeing miracles, and having prayers answered, then perhaps we need to be like Jesus in some other ways too. And we can.

It was around a decade ago that I had a life-changing experience whilst reading though the fifth chapter of Luke's Gospel. But there had been a quiet, at times latent, yearning deep within my heart for many years.

As a young Christian I would read through the Gospels, and would note the way that Jesus at times vanished from the scene. Where was he? – he was in the wilderness, or the desert, or on a lonely mountainside, spending time with his Father. And as I read, I would consider the intercourse and dialogue that took place during those times – and I wished that I could have a similar experience. But it never happened.

The years passed. I had come to Christ in October 1965, and it was early in the twenty-first century that I sat in my study reading through Luke, when the Holy Spirit spoke just two words to me that changed everything. Just two words! As I read verse 16 of chapter 5, something happened. I was reading from the New International Version at the time, and it reads –

'And Jesus often went to solitary places and prayed.'

So simple. But I felt compelled to stop and prayerfully hover over the verse. 'Jesus' – our great example. 'Often', means 'often'. 'Went to solitary places' means he went to places where there were no distractions, and he could be alone. 'And prayed' meant 'and prayed'. Simple. I imagined Jesus going out to deserted places and up into mountains where he was absolutely alone, except for his Father. I wondered what they had spoken about, and how much was talking and how much was listening. And again I felt that quiet longing in my heart for such times myself – but they never happened.

"Schedule it." The words seemed so clear, and in fact they not only impacted me with clarity, but also conveyed a practical response. My heart leapt – I could do what Jesus had done. He had spent hours alone with his Father, and I could do just the same. It had never happened before. Of course it had never happened before, because I was always too busy. But how did I manage to spend time with people, patients, friends and family? By scheduling it. Times with patients were placed in my appointment book, and whether it was for ten minutes or three hours (yes, occasionally some treatments did need a three hour appointment), it was reserved for them. And likewise in my personal diary, time was booked out for people. If someone wanted to see me during that time – then 'tough', because it was already promised to the person, or people, booked in. This was exciting, and I hastened to explain to Wendy what the Lord had shown me, and of the practical significance.

The next morning I was up in good time and, having arrived at the surgery, turned on the computer and brought up the appointment calendar for the following twelve months. I crossed off one day a month as 'holiday', and wrote 'P&F' for prayer and fasting in my personal diary. As I was self-employed, it was unpaid leave, but it was necessary because I now had scheduled appointments with my Heavenly Father.

The first of these days arrived, and I was quietly anticipating something wonderful. What had happened when Jesus met with his father for quality time alone? Was there an audible voice at times, a vision or other manifestation of his presence, or... Surely days alone with the Lord would be remarkable indeed.

But there is a war on – did you know? Though Jesus has come to bring life in abundant measure (John 10:10) – and I can certainly testify to how the Lord increased my own quality of life by changing an unfulfilled atheist into a very fulfilled Christian – the same verse tells us that Satan comes to kill and to steal and to destroy. He is opposed to God, God's people, God's Word, God's purposes, and everything else that is a part of the Lord's big plan. I think this explains some of my experiences on the first day of this new season of fasting and praying. Let me tell you about it.

I drove to the North Norfolk coast until I found a remote spot. I had with me my Bible, a notebook and a pen. I did *not* have a newspaper, and I turned my mobile phone *OFF*. There was a small area of waste land where I parked my car, and after sitting and reading and just worshipping God for a while, I stepped out of the car and made for the beach. The sea had gone out for what looked like miles, and I walked through the grass dunes down onto the beach. However, it was not beach, but slimy mudflats, and I immediately started skidding around and very nearly fell over. I made it back to the low sandy cliffs, and found my shoes were covered in mud. Surely it would be better to walk along the path that ran along the cliff edge, and so I turned along the track known as the

North Norfolk Coastal trail, and – was almost knocked over by two cyclists. "Sorry mate," they muttered, and ten minutes later the experience was repeated. I dived for cover and made my way back to the car, where I spent some time reading, praying, praising and worshipping the Creator of oceans, dunes, grassy cliffs and mudflats. After quite some time I decided that I would return to my home and spend the rest of the day in our summerhouse at the top of the garden. However, I had not driven too far when I realised there was a problem with the car, and found that a nail from the wasteland was firmly embedded in my front near side tyre. So the wheel had to be changed and the tyre repaired. Was that the end of my catalogue of disasters? I'm not really adept at anything mechanical, and a week later, returning from a stint of baby-sitting around midnight, the car gave an incredible shudder and the front near side wheel departed from the car. OK – so I'm not really very good at putting wheels on! And that resulted in us sitting in the dark for an hour in the middle of the night waiting for roadside assistance, and then having to pay for a new wheel – and another new tyre. As I mentioned, there is a war on.

A month later I headed to a different place on the North Norfolk coast, found a cliff-top car park in the centre of a large village, and walked down cliff paths to the sandy beach where, under an overcast sky, families were playing by the sea. I walked north, and continued doing so until there was no one in sight. Jesus went to *solitary* places, where there were no distractions. I had just my Bible, notebook and pen, and my mobile was turned off. Walking by the waves as they crashed onto the beach, I could shout – and I mean *SHOUT* – my praises to God as I lifted my hands to heaven and worshipped him. After some time I headed back to the cliffs, where boulders were lying together with tangled sections of metal and concrete sea-defences that had themselves long fallen victim to the onslaught that periodically causes disaster along our eastern coast. I sat on a section of weathered concrete and opened my Bible. After maybe thirty minutes of reading, I closed my eyes and asked the Lord that I might know his presence with me. Yes, *know* his presence, because I seemed to have gained so little from my scheduled day one month earlier. My eyes were closed, but I was aware of the light as the sun emerged from behind the clouds, and at the same time I felt the warmth on the back of my neck. I enjoyed the light and the warmth, and started opening my heart to the Lord, sharing how I felt about so much that was happening in my life. I opened my eyes. So where was the sun? Why the light and warmth, when the sky was, if anything, more overcast than before?

I again asked the Lord to bless me with his presence. I realised, of course, that he is always with us. 'In him we live and move and have our being' (Acts 17:28), but there are those times when he 'comes down' (Genesis 11:5 would be just one example of this), or 'fills people' (Acts 2:4 would be just one example of this) or in some other way gives us an *experience* of his presence. I closed my eyes and again there was an unmistakable sense of light and warmth, which I enjoyed as I worshipped the King of kings, my Heavenly Father. And yet on opening my eyes a little later, the sky was still overcast and the sun obscured behind significant cloud.

I appreciate that much of this is subjective, but that is the nature of relationship. I sense the Lord's presence quite often, and rather than spend time seeking to prove or somehow convince others, I shall simply continue to enjoy it. The word of God speaks for itself concerning such matters.

And for most of the past ten years or so, I have taken one day a month to simply get alone with God. It is *scheduled*, and I cannot overemphasise the importance of this. *SCHEDULE IT.* Write it in your diary. Buy a diary! Maybe you use an electronic diary; if so, use it for scheduling time with the Lord. Use it, daily and constantly! Ask the Lord to make his presence known. Worship him, praise him, open your heart, and listen. More recently I have been taking mornings and afternoons, but a few weeks ago I felt the Lord speak to me and emphasise *days*. So days are being scheduled again in the diary.

It's not a case of Brownie points for being good. It's not rewards for good works. Every good thing we receive from the Lord is a gift, and of grace. Undeserved, unmerited favour. It is simply about relationship.

Return for a minute to the story of the two men at the beginning of this chapter. Did we help Tom because he had done something to deserve our help? No. Did we stop helping him because he did something to 'not deserve' our help? No. It was all about relationship. And likewise with Robin. Please do not take this illustration too far when applying it to God and us, because he is obviously far more gracious than Wendy and me. But, relationship is so important, and as Wendy and I so often say to one another, "It's not what we say, but what we *do*!" If I love the Lord, I will spend time with him. If I love him a lot, I shall prioritise such times. Perhaps even *schedule* them to ensure that they happen.

Relationship. Time with the Lord. Priority. Schedule it. *SO GET YOUR DIARY OUT!*

## In Summary

If you know how much the Lord loves you, then you will really love him too. Love finds expression in action and conduct. It results in spending time with the one you love. It results in enjoying the relationship you have with him, and from this, flows prayer that is led by the Spirit himself – and that is prayer that gets answered.

\* \* \*

*'Jesus often withdrew to lonely places and prayed.'*
Luke 5:16 (NIV)

# Chapter 24

# Please Dad...

"You do not have because you do not ask." we read in James 4:2. Clearly, the Lord expects us to ask him for things when we pray. Jesus himself had a lot to say about asking and receiving, especially in John 14 and 15, and also in the Sermon on the Mount, where he taught us "Ask, and you will receive." (Matthew 7:7). So, we should ask.

And yet so many people have told me that their prayers are rarely answered. They seem to be sceptical as to whether I am telling the truth when I give examples of answered prayer, and sometimes proceed to give me examples of unanswered prayer. Why is this?

I myself have been bewildered at times, when prayer requests that I have felt to be more than reasonable, and usually based on revelation in scripture of what the Lord wants, have not been answered. I consider some of the reasons for this in a later chapter.

I have already explained that it is God's will that we should be part of his family. In one sense all people are 'the offspring of God' in that he created us. However, the Bible is quite clear that not everyone is part of the family of God in the way that he desires. In John 8:44 Jesus tells some of the religious leaders, "You belong to your father, the devil..." and in Acts 13:10, a sorcerer called Elymas is told by Paul, "You are a child of the devil..." Clearly there is a very real sense in which God is *not* the father of some people, if the devil is their father. I have explained in an earlier chapter how anyone of us can become a child of God, and know him as our Father; in fact, we can know him with such intimacy that we can call him Abba, *Dad*, we are told in Romans 8:15.

* * *

So now we have a heavenly Dad. We are invited to deepen our relationship with him, enjoy him, get caught up in his purposes and work with him. So what do we do? How do we pray?

"Please make the sun shine."

"Please give good weather."

"Please help me pay these bills."

"Please make this other person different so that life is easier for me."

"Please give me a husband."

"Please give me a holiday."

"Please make the children behave."

Little children *want*! Babies want feeding, and certainly let their parents know about it. They also want their nappy changing from time to time, because a full one makes life uncomfortable, and let the parents know that too. There is an innate selfishness in each one of us from birth whereby we are primarily, if not solely, concerned with getting our needs met.

Only the new birth brings a new life, with new values and motives. However, we have 'behaviour patterns' which often need to be unlearnt before we can properly proceed with our new life. Let me explain.

We are born, and grow up, selfish. Life is all about me, me, ME! And then we have an encounter with Christ and are born-again. Wow – it's a new life, because I'm a new person. But the old ways, the old behaviour patterns, are still there. So *what* do I pray? "Please make the sun shine, please give good weather, please help me pay these bills...."

Have you ever prayed any of these prayers? Maybe. Were you wrong to do so? Maybe. Should your praying be different from that? Yes. Should you recite the Lord's Prayer each day? No – but looking at it is a good place to start.

The disciples asked Jesus how they should pray, and his response is probably the most helpful teaching on the subject that you will ever find. The disciples asked Jesus about prayer because they wanted to get it right. Jesus' teaching was designed to help them get it right. How about us?

*Our Father.* We address God as our Father. That is who he is if we have been born again. We are part of his family. He is Abba, or Dad. This language invites us to be familiar, intimate, and close. There is no need for religious language – my children don't use religious language when speaking to me. There is no need for using strange voices and intonations, sing-songing or whispering – my children don't address me in that manner! There is no requirement that we always add 'in Jesus Name'. He's our Dad, so he will take these things 'as read'. We can do so too.

*Hallowed be your name.* May your name be holy. Hey – he's our dad, but he is also *the Almighty God.* He can do *anything*! Know that, please – my Dad can do *absolutely anything.* And there is still no need for archaic words, prayer formulae, strange voices, whispering, etc. What is your concept of God? Does he like strange archaic words and whispering voices and strange ways of saying things? Why should he? I am created in the image of God and I don't want that from *my* children. Be real.

But if he is God, and he certainly is, then he is also to be worshipped. There is no conflict here with him being our father. I worship him – I raise my hands to him (God's people have always done that, even if it is not usual in some churches) and I sing to him, and sometimes shout to him, and sometimes dance for joy as part of my expression of praise. I might stand, kneel, sit, or simply be walking beside the sea – but I worship him. I really worship him, because he is my Creator and my God.

*Your kingdom come and your will be done.* Do you see the priorities? 'Please give me this, and please give me that' really does not make any showing yet in Jesus teaching. So what does? God's kingdom and God's will. So – how do you pray?

"How can I be more effective for your kingdom?"

"How can I serve You best?"

"Which church should I be part of?"

"Please give me opportunities to extend your kingdom today."

"Please give me people I can speak to in an encouraging manner."

"Please help me be quiet and listen to those from whom I can learn."

"Please help me see my failings, repent of them and be more like Jesus."

"Please show me your will for my future career."

"Please show me your will for where I should live."

"Please help me to be altogether more 'God-centred' and less self-centred."

＊ ＊ ＊

Let's just pause and recap on what I'm saying. Some people I speak to are sceptical about answered prayer, and are surprised when I give numerous examples of God doing just that in my life and the lives of many people I know. I suspect that their concept of prayer is to go straight into, 'Please do this, God' and 'Please do that, God' and 'I want this, God' – and of course, quite a number of people expressing scepticism are not born-again, and have a different concept of God than I do, or as he is revealed to us in the Bible. Their God is not the Christian God we read about in the Bible. 'Prayer' is an expression of relationship, and not just a shopping list of 'wants' presented to heaven. Maybe some people in Jesus' day had a similar wrong concept of prayer, and his teaching on the subject was to help them understand. He taught that we approach God as *Dad*, but that we also worship him. He is so accessible to his children, but can also do *absolutely anything*. Because I love him, those things that are important to *him* will take priority over those things that are important to *me*. So I will be praying for his kingdom to come to earth more widely, to be extended into more people's lives, that I might have opportunities to help in this, and so on.

\* \* \*

*Give us this day...*

Now we come to 'Please.' We take so much for granted, and especially so in the western world. We do not ask for food because it is plentiful – and we do not thank God for it either. I can remember when, at University, I became engaged to be married, and my fiancée and I started thinking of how we would live when married. One matter is still clear in my memory – we would give thanks for our food. God's people did so in Old Testament times and in New Testament times, and Jesus, our great example, always gave thanks when he 'broke bread'. We decided we would too, and when she joined me from time to time in our hostel refectory, we would pause and thank God in prayer before eating. Maybe others would stare, maybe others did not understand – but our basic necessities of life are gifts from God, and we decided we would thank him for them. In reminding ourselves that he was the source, we would also remember to ask. "Please – give us our daily bread and all the other things we need for life." There are things we *need* in order to live, and without them we are of little use to God or man. So let's ask him, and thank him.

Jesus said that we 'live by every word that proceeds from the mouth of God,' Matthew 4:4. I want to live, and therefore I need to hear God. So let us ask him to speak, and as we go through life, let's listen. Hearing God creates faith, by which we live.

*And forgive us our trespasses, as we forgive those who trespass against us.* Do you ever sin? Then you need to be forgiven! All sin is against God, because he is the one who has told us not to. Sin offends God and messes us up. And it messes up others. Jesus took our punishment at Calvary, so all we need to do is ask forgiveness, show our sincerity by turning from such behaviour (repentance), and forgive others who might sin against us. Where we have wronged others, we need to go to them and to do our best to put matters right. Sometimes restitution is needed.

In Matthew 18 we read of a man who was let off an enormous debt by a king. He then refused to forgive a man who owed him a puny amount. The lesson for us? If we fail to forgive those who wrong us, then we have no appreciation of just how much we have been forgiven by God. Maybe we need to check whether we have really come to God in the first place?

We want our prayers answered? Then sin needs to be dealt with whenever it occurs, in us or in others. 'If I regard sin in my heart, the Lord will not hear me,' reads Psalm 66:18.

Sin messes us up – so don't. But we do. So come to Jesus in sincere repentance, and he will obliterate your sin and restore you completely. Totally unmessed up again. Totally restored. Squeaky clean. Likewise, if we fail to forgive, we are messed up, and need to repent of *that* sin. As I have said elsewhere, some of the saddest and loneliest people I know are those who have not repented of sin, and also those who have not forgiven others. Ask forgiveness, and be forgiven.

*Lead us not into temptation, but deliver us from evil.* We have been forgiven our sin, and have ourselves forgiven others – then please Lord, we don't want to go there again. We ask that we might not find ourselves in situations where we are liable to fall into sin again or 'unforgive' others. Likewise, we ask that the Lord will give grace that we might withstand any temptation from within ourselves as well as protecting us from attacks of the world, the flesh and the devil in the hostile environment of a fallen creation.

*For Thine is the kingdom, the power and the glory* This is key to living a life in meaningful relationship to the Lord in which we can expect, not just to see prayers answered, but to know the reality of our God in every realm of life and to experience the abundant life that Jesus himself speaks of in John 10:10. Are we primarily concerned for the glory of our God and Saviour in all that we do? This is indeed a matter of vital importance, and for those of us who want to see our prayers answered within the context of the kingdom being extended, the power of God being manifested, and the glory of Jesus increasing daily, we need to see that the glory goes to Jesus – not us. I will write on this in the next chapter.

\* \* \*

'*Lord, teach us to pray.*' Luke 11:1

'*Our Father...*' Luke 11:2

# Chapter 25

## *Thine be the Glory!*

"Look at me! Look at me!" shouted our young grandson, as grandsons do. I think he was rather like me at his age, and probably like you too!

It might seem excusable in a child of three or four, but it also occurs, though in a more subtle, and often more practised form, in adults. Many years ago I read the book *Preachers and Preaching* by Dr. Martyn Lloyd-Jones. He tells the story of a man who was a famous preacher in his day and in his country. People flocked to meetings where he spoke, and there would be a great sense of anticipation and excitement as he did so. When would he 'do it'? Do what? – well, this man was famous for his magnificent hair, divided by a long parting which extended down the back of his head. It was immaculate, and at some point in his preaching – but only once, and towards the end of his sermon – he would appear to become so passionate and animated in what he was saying, that he would slowly spin round a complete 360°. Just once per preach. And everyone would see that fine parting! He always did it. He was a showman as well as a preacher – and who do you think got the fame, the recognition, the glory? Jesus – or the preacher?

Reading the above, you might rightly consider that to be a gross case of vainglory. But it can be far more subtle – yet still be taking glory for oneself when we should be concerned with pointing to Jesus and glorifying him.

The issue is this – the work of the Spirit is to glorify Jesus, and we are invited to work with the Spirit. But that involves us glorifying Jesus too. The Spirit never points to himself, or to us – only to Jesus. We must do likewise. If we fail in this area, the Spirit is liable to withdraw, and he is the One who answers prayer with miracles.

Our significance, true identity and destiny lie in our relationship with God. In the beginning, Adam and Eve were quite content with being the people the Lord had made them to be – children of God. They did not desire more, and enjoyed life on earth, and fellowship with their Father.

But here lies the problem – sin occurred, and I do not need to elaborate on what happened. One of the consequences was that man lost his relationship with God. I explained in the last chapter that people are not born into this world as 'children of God' because that was lost at the Fall, and the result is that since then, people do not have a Father/son relationship with God, and have no true sense of identity and destiny. Without our true identity, we are unfulfilled, and look for satisfaction elsewhere. We think we shall find fulfilment in a particular identity – the important person, the wise person, the qualified person, the humorous person, the family person... Our quest for identity starts in babyhood, when we like to be 'the star', with all eyes on us. Any satisfaction this brings is short-lived, and we continue to strive for fulfilment. The world, the flesh and the devil seem to promise so much – but none really delivers. And so we continue striving for fulfilment, seeking that niche and that identity where we *will* be satisfied. But it just does not happen, and even the 'top dog' wants to get higher still.

In coming to Jesus and being born again into the family of God, we find our true identity. I was created to be a child of God – and now I have arrived. Personally, I believe the biggest difference Christ has made to my life is that he brought me fulfilment. An unfulfilled Barrie became a fulfilled Barrie.

But, prior to our conversion, we had built up behaviour patterns, some of which related to our unfulfilled state. These need to be unlearned!

## Status

In the family of God, the Church, we all have the same status – 'child of God'. We have different giftings and callings, but we still have the same status – child of God. Some have more authority, but we all have the same status – child of God. We need to find fulfilment in being a child of God, whilst also using and developing our gifting, and moving in the call that God has put on our life.

But so often the church mimics the world. The behaviour patterns developed in the world, which people believe will lead to fulfilment, have no place in God's family. The career structure within so many churches, both the traditional and the new churches, is only too obvious. And a career structure attracts career Christians. My own experience has been largely in the new churches, where there has sometimes been a 'culture of leadership', but I am sure that this is no less so within the more traditional branches and denominations of the Church. Culture of leadership? The leaders become so important relative to the other church members, that there are 'the leaders' and 'the rest'. The leaders 'do the stuff', and the rest listen. The leaders go to special meetings and conferences, and the rest pay for them. If insecure, the leaders discuss all church matters behind closed doors, and the rest have to pay attention (for a while) to their decisions. New people coming into the church are assessed (probably unknown to the people themselves) as either 'leadership material' or 'not leadership material'.

There are those who aspire to leadership because they want importance – and they work towards it. 'Hey, look at me!' There are those who were used to a leadership rôle in the world, and expect no less in their church. Once in it, they are immoveable. 'Hey, look at me!' There are those who have always been 'the little people' in the world systems, and unexpectedly find themselves in a position of leadership in the church. They love it, and will never relinquish it. 'Hey, look at me!' And there are those, some in leadership and some not, who are very contented where they are, but striving to move in the calling God has placed on their lives, whilst developing their gifting.

One of the problems resulting from the above, is that those with gifting in the areas of pastoring, preaching, and teaching, and yet who are politically unacceptable to the leaders, local or regional, can be seen as a threat to insecure people already in leadership (and believe me, they exist) and who want to be the ones who 'wear the badge' and who 'do the stuff'.

I could elaborate at length here, but the underlying problem is the unfulfilled and insecure person wanting importance – glory! We are all liable to slip into it, and it *kills* the true work of the Church. There is only one person who is important, and his name is Jesus. There is only one person who should really be noticed, and his name is Jesus. There is only one person who people should be directed to look at, and his name is Jesus.

The work of the Holy Spirit is to glorify Jesus. Jesus himself said, "When he, the Spirit of truth comes, he will glorify me." (John 16:13,14.) We are called to be fellow-labourers in the work of the gospel (1 Corinthians 3:9), working with the Holy Spirit, but if our agenda is different from his, we may well find that he withdraws. However, this may go completely unnoticed in many churches. It has rightly been said that if the Holy Spirit totally withdrew from the Church, most churches would continue with their respective programmes, because they were not involved with the Holy Spirit in the first place.

## Striving or Contented?

Within the systems of this world, there is so often a restless striving for position and status. However, God's people are told in Philippians 4:11 to be contented. This obviously does not mean that we are to be contented about a world full of immorality, injustice and idolatry, heading for destruction. We are to preach the gospel. Nor are we to be contented with our gifting remaining as it is – we are to use our gifting by serving, and to develop what the Lord has given us for the growth of His Church. But we are to be content with our *status* as a child of God.

In using our gifting, and seeking to move in the call of God on our lives, we glorify Jesus. But there is a bonus for those serving in this way – fulfilment and contentment. I appreciate that many churches do not give opportunity for everyone to use their gifting, or move in their call, and I will write a little about this next.

## Launching Out – for the glory of God

If we are going to see the Lord get glory through the sick being healed, then we need to pray for them. If he is to receive glory by miracles being performed, then we need to perform them. In other words, for his glory, we need to launch out. We also need to encourage one another, and to make room for each other to do this. In Romans 12:10 we are told that we should 'prefer one another' in honour.

Wendy and I were in the same church for twenty-five years, during which time we grew from around thirty to a number many, many times that, and comprising several churches. In the early days, each person was encouraged to discover their gifting and call, and to participate in the meetings and church-life generally. But there is a limit to how many people can speak in a large meeting (and our meetings were certainly growing in size in those days), though many can participate without necessarily having an up-front role. There are those who set out the chairs, the PA team, the ushers, and so on. Yet everybody does need to identify and use his or her gifting within the life of the church, and the New Testament suggests that most people, if not all, have an active part to play in the *meetings* of the church.

The larger the meeting, the more difficult it is for each person to take part, except in joining in the praise and worship, and saying a hearty 'Amen' to good preaching and good praying. In the larger meetings, it is necessary to have leadership by an individual or a team, but care needs to be taken that this does not become the expectation for every other meeting. There needs to be teaching, encouragement, and opportunity for each person to identify and use the gifting God has given them.

What is your gifting? Are you using it? There need to be meetings in the church where people can find and use their gifting, even though to some extent this might involve experimenting. There was a time when the meetings in the church where Wendy and I were members were either 'Sunday morning meetings' of around one hundred and fifty people, 'Sunday evening meetings' of around forty where there was prayer and one or two people would give very fluent and articulate prophecies, or smaller 'home groups' where there was a weekly Bible Study or prayer meeting or social time. Where could people discover and use their gifts, as most of us felt too timid to launch out in front of a large congregation, or follow the polished prophesiers of Sunday evenings, and it was 'out of place' in the very structured Bible Study, prayer meeting or social events? I prayed about it, and felt the Lord was giving me a plan. I spoke to the church leaders, and with their permission shared my thoughts briefly at one of the church meetings. I wanted five people – no more than five, but not less either – who felt a desire to move in the gifts, and who could commit to six weekly meetings of one hour each. But commitment *meant* commitment – no dropping out unless dead! Nobody volunteered, and so back at my home in prayer, I asked the Lord who he would have gather together, and having received names, I approached five men in the church who each seemed to wholeheartedly embrace the idea. Most had hardly been operating in the gifts at all, ever, and one older man had on occasions in the dim and distant past, prophesied. I too had launched out a little on occasion.

We met together for one hour each week. We could talk, drink coffee, whatever we liked until 7.30 p.m., and then we stopped and simply asked the Lord to give us gifts, and the necessary boldness to use them. And at 8.30 p.m. we stopped, and people went home, or stayed for more coffee. But the time from 7.30 p.m. to 8.30 p.m. was sacrosanct. We decided it was quite OK to experiment, and to launch out with anything we felt the Lord might have given us. Even praise and prayer was banned, except for laying hands on one another and asking the Spirit to come and impart a gift, and for the person to use it. We could laugh at ourselves, but not at each other – only *with* each other.

There were incentives in the form of goals. After two weeks, each of us would try and launch out with one of the gifts in the Bible Study or prayer meeting or whatever their small group was doing that week, regardless of this being outside the group's 'comfort zone'. After four weeks, each of us would try and launch out in the Sunday evening meeting attended by around forty people, and where the two or three people who seemed 'quite good at prophesying' would probably launch out first. And after six weeks, our goal was to launch out with a gift in the main Sunday morning meeting.

What happened? Firstly, just one person missed just one meeting, and so there was commitment that led to bonding and mutual encouragement. At every meeting, there were gifts. During the six weeks, every person moved in the gifts (especially messages in tongues, interpretations, prophesy and visions) at some time, and several people did every week. There were times when the Spirit of God seemed to fall on us in unusual ways, and some or all would fall to the floor, either in silence, or on occasions, with laughter. Can one call it 'holy laughter'? I believe so. Most goals were not achieved, though one of us achieved all three. There was hushed and excited anticipation in at least five people in the church one Sunday morning as one man walked to the microphone and said, "I believe the Lord has given me something that I want to deliver in a prophetic manner." There were many shouts of 'Amen' as he finished.

It would have been easy to pat one another on the back and say 'Well done', and to some extent we did encourage one another in this way, but – we gave the glory to God. We wanted to meet with him, even though we were of ourselves unworthy. God is gracious, and he delights to bless us. We praised him. We spoke about what he was doing. And at the end of it, we were emboldened to launch out a little more in giving people prophetic words and praying for the sick, etc. And in all these things, we were mindful to give the glory to Jesus.

Launch out. Make room for one another to launch out, and encourage those who do, always giving the glory to the Lord. Especially if you are a leader, consider how you can encourage your people to find and use their gifting.

## Anointing

Who does what in the church? The answer to this is often found in a 'system' in the more traditional churches, where in order to teach or preach, one has to do a course, maybe attend a college, and sometimes even have a University degree. (A man I once knew said that the churches were getting colder by degrees!). But the leadership can make way for people.

In the newer churches, there is a feeling that they have broken free from the restrictions of the more historic churches – and yet they develop their own. Church politics involving regional and local leadership very often determines 'who does what' in the churches. And so many 'leaders' have University degrees.

The church Wendy and I used to attend was blessed with lovely people, including the leaders. The regional leaders were, I am sure, godly men, though people at our level did not really rub shoulders much with them. But we all make mistakes, and I hope I will be forgiven for relating what I believe was an error of judgment by our local and regional leaders. It happened quite a long time ago, but is helpful in making an important point about church life.

As I have already written, our church started with around thirty people, and most of them took quite an active rôle in meetings and in other ways. There was much prayer for many years, and then it seemed as though heaven opened. Although we were only one of seven churches in a small market town of around four thousand inhabitants, unchurched people started coming to evangelistic meetings where they gave their hearts and lives to the Lord. One year we had fifty-two people professing conversion, and before long we had grown to around three hundred, had outgrown our venue four times, eventually buying and converting an old coach station. The leaders decided to join a wider 'movement', and I think it is fair to say that we lost much of our autonomy. At one point the church went through a difficult time, and the regional apostolic team told the elders to stand down. They did so, reluctantly, and were replaced with a leadership team of ten men, even though there were only around seventy people attending services and the membership stood at significantly less. It was decided that each of the ten men would preach on successive Sundays. One Sunday, the speaker was a man with much pastoral gifting, but with around zero ability to preach. He droned on for twenty-five minutes or so before saying 'Amen'. He then looked at his watch, and muttered, 'Oh dear, I have another twenty minutes yet. Now, what shall I talk about? Um. I think I'll tell you about...' and the congregation sighed, closed their eyes and rested their chins back on their chests as he continued to drone for a further twenty minutes. Around the same time, another man was told by the leaders, "You have the anointing of an elder, but you can't be one because of your past." But it was *church politics*, and not his past, which really overruled the anointing of God.

The anointing of God is critical. Read the latter half of 1 Corinthians 1 and you will find that God does not choose too many people who are wise and noble by worldly standards. He chooses whom he will, and he indicates and equips them by anointing them with his Spirit. This might be a somewhat subjective matter, but the Lord is well able to make clear whom he has anointed, and indeed, whom he has not. A man who wins souls and brings people into the kingdom is anointed as an evangelist, whether or not he has qualifications or training. Likewise with preaching, teaching, administration and every other ministry in the church. And this brings glory to God, because the anointing is the work of the Spirit, and he is directed by Jesus, who is Head of the Church. The Spirit glorifies Jesus – that is what he does! So let the Spirit determine, and make room for those that the Lord has chosen, even if it means church-ordained leaders standing back.

To summarise this, we can say that God's anointing is God's appointing. He is the one who should be determining all church decisions, and when we get that right, we will find that prayer is increasingly answered, the churches will grow and Jesus will be glorified.

Wendy and I were part of the church I have mentioned for twenty-five years, and loved to see the Lord at work there so much of the time. They were great people, committed to serving God. We really felt that, not only had the Lord placed us in that church, but that he had placed us in a godly church where we were blessed, and also given opportunity to use the gifting he had given to us. I was not one of the 'in people' because I did not dot my 'i's and cross my 't's quite like the leaders and the movement we had joined. But I was asked to preach every few months, and Wendy and I had a cell group meeting in our home. A number of younger men, usually professional and managerial, were given space to preach, teach and pastor, and some became elders.

## Give the Church Back to Jesus!

But a vision for 'church' – church where Jesus really is Head, where the Spirit really does lead, and where each person is encouraged to use their gifting and move in their call – was etched deeply into my understanding of God's will for us, from my early days as a believer. How can church politics over-rule Jesus Headship of the church, or the Spirit's anointing and leading? But quite often it does.

It was September 2008, and one morning in the early hours, I woke up having had a vivid dream. I have written of this in my first book, *There Must Be More to Life Than This!* and mentioned it in Part One of this book. However, it is relevant to give a little more detail here. Because of the nature and intensity of the dream, Wendy and I felt very strongly that the Lord was calling us to start something new, but we were so used to our old church. All our friends were there! So who would join us? – we did not want to take anyone from the church we were a part of at that time, or any other church. And so we dragged our heels, and eventually left in May 2011. We told people in our old church, which was several miles from our home, not to join us, and the two of us sat alone on a sofa in our sitting room and worshipped, praised, read scripture, broke bread, and asked God to lead us.

Although we did not publicise what we were doing, and live in a rather rural location, others came, though to date 29 is the most we have had gathered together. But we want to **give the church back to Jesus, and we want the Holy Spirit to lead.** I could not tell you who will be preaching or teaching next Sunday – or prophesying, giving a message in tongues, a testimony..... If someone feels they have a word, we can programme them in – but the Spirit might lead us differently. Sometimes it seems we get off track, and then we need to get back 'in the Spirit' again, though this is done through leadership with a consensus agreement.

In honour, preferring one another? We make room for each other. No-one comes determined to speak, but they might come prepared to. We tend to make way for one another, and the person who wants to 'do their thing' and get some glory, is usually engaged in conversation later, where our vision is explained to them! Those who want to be stars tend to move on. We want a fully functioning Body, and that means that the more vocal and experienced people have an attitude of, 'No – after you please'.

But how can *you* find a church or fellowship where you can seek to glorify Jesus by using your gift? Speak to your church leaders about this, and you might be surprised to find them making opportunities for you. But for those in a church where everything is done by the leaders, and you will only ever be given chores to do, there are three options –

1. Stay quiet, and lose your gifting. Remember the man who did not use his talent in Matthew 25. But if you feel strongly that the Lord wants you in that church, pray fervently that he will open a door for you to use your gifting there.

2. Find a para-church fellowship where there *are* opportunities to exercise your gifting and ministry. I am quite involved with the Full Gospel Businessmen's Fellowship, and we have meetings which are open for ministry. We welcome people, and there are other fellowships that do too. Ask around. Google it. Or find like-minded people and come together to seek God.

3. Ask the Lord if you are in the right church. I am where I am because that is where the Lord has clearly shown that he wants me. And likewise with my previous church nearly thirty years ago. If you keep looking for the right church for you, and you continue moving from church to church, it will lead to you being known as a church-hopper, spiritual gypsy or roaming catholic. And rightly so, because you will keep moving on. But if God shows you the place he has for you – and make sure it *is* God – then you are well on the way to finding your

destiny. And when there, stay there and glorify Him by exercising your gift. The Lord builds his church from living stones, not rolling stones.

## But remember...

But remember – the glory must always go to Jesus. This cannot be overemphasised, and regardless of church, fellowship, gifting, calling, ministry or anything else, if we try to take some of the glory, the Spirit is likely to withdraw. We work with Him, and prayer that is heard and answered is part of the process of building the Church and extending the kingdom.

I know a man who seems greatly used of God, and whenever I meet him, he tells me of words of knowledge he has received, and of how he has prayed with so many people. He's so spiritual, mightily used, so sensitive to the Spirit – but I find I am admiring him more than Jesus in these stories. When speaking of how the Lord has used us in these ways, we need to be careful not to leave people admiring us!

A lady evangelist sat in my dental chair. She was visiting from the States, and for someone wanting dental treatment, her jaw never stopped moving as she told me about her ministry. And then she said, "My dentist back home just talks about Jesus all day long. Right Barrie – how many people have you talked to about the Lord today?" I wanted the surgery floor to open up and swallow me. I felt so small and useless. Clearly this lady, and her dentist, were real stars in the kingdom, people who would be mega-commended on their arrival in heaven – but I think maybe this lady was more of a star than Jesus in her conversation.

"So I said to the Lord... and the Lord said to me... and I said to the Lord... and he said to me..." Yawn, shuffle, 'where is this going?' I suppose there are times when I get alone with God and converse. My part is usually praise and worship as I wander along a lonely seashore or heathland, but I do have questions for Him at times. However, I do not have lengthy conversations with God that are to be shared with other Christians. Maybe you don't know such people, but I've come across a few who like to relate such conversations ad nauseam, ad infinitum. I do not think I am really an impatient man these days, but I wish they would go away. Am I supposed to be impressed? And who is getting the glory? So, just in case you are such a person – think about it!

## Increasing and decreasing

Most believers are familiar with the words of John the Baptist when he said that Jesus must increase, but he must decrease (John 3:30). Up until a certain point, John was centre stage, preaching repentance, baptising hundreds, maybe thousands, and gaining many followers. And then he met Jesus, and everything changed. "He's the One," he said. "Follow him." He said that he was unworthy to untie even Jesus' sandals, and in fact, from the moment he met Jesus, he started fading away as he pointed people to Christ. What a lesson for us. We can be slow to learn lessons, and even slower to unlearn behaviour patterns – but from the time we first meet Jesus we need to decrease as we point people to him. And as we work with the Spirit, as a co-labourer in the work of the kingdom, so we will find our walk with God becomes closer, our life more fulfilling, and prayers about both the small everyday matters as well as the biggies concerning miracles and saved souls and kingdom extension, will be heard and answered.

\* \* \*

'Not unto us, O LORD, not unto us, but to
Your name give glory.' **Psalm 115:1**

'When He, the Spirit of truth, has come....
He will glorify Me.' **John 16:13,14**

# Chapter 26

## Pleasing God

In Ephesians 5:10 we are told to 'find out those things that please the Lord.' The reason for this is clear – so that we can do them and please God. When a couple marry, they usually try and find out the things that please their partner. I heard the story of a newly wed couple, where the wife soon realised that her husband enjoyed curry. So she gave him a wonderful surprise dinner one evening – Mulligatawny soup, followed by hot curry, with ginger pudding for dessert. Maybe a slight case of overkill! But she wanted to do what pleased him, because she loved him.

In this chapter, I have written of some of the things that I believe particularly please God. It is not an exhaustive list, and I am sure that some people will have other things higher on their agenda. However, I believe the areas of life I have covered here are important in living a life pleasing to the Lord, a life in which we can expect to find our prayers answered and see miracles.

Not that we have prayers answered as a reward, still less payment, for pleasing God or doing good or keeping rules – it is all about *relationship*. We try and please those we love, purely in order to do just that – please them. In order to receive something back? No – it's just because we love them. But my experience tells me that those people I have known who have lived to please God – people of prayer, kindness, mercy, generosity, holiness and so forth would appear to be closer to the Lord, and receiving from him in a way that most others have not.

## Rôle Model on Father

Glen (not his real name) received a merit at school for writing an essay, and was allowed to take the work home for his parents to read. The title of the essay was *The Man I Admire Most*, and he proudly presented it to his father who immediately started to read the composition. Before long, he was avidly devouring it, with an ever-increasing smile on his face. Suddenly, the smile vanished. He paused, and then continued reading with a look of incredulity. In fact, it was the father who told me about it. "The man he admired most," he said, with the hint of a smile, "is in his late thirties, and is a practising Christian. He enjoys red wine, and when he can afford it, good food in good restaurants. He is amusing, and makes Glen smile a lot, as well as being successful within his profession." Glen's father Ken continued, "I assumed that I would be the man Glen admired most, and started reading that into his story. 'It's me, it's me', I thought, and then I read the words, 'And he drives a white Lotus sports car, just like James Bond'. And suddenly I realised that it wasn't me – it was *you*, Barrie!"

Yes, I drove a white Lotus Esprit just like James Bond in the film *The Spy Who Loved Me*, which had been released a few years earlier, and the fact that I had made rather a mess of my life at that particular time was totally ignored by Glen – I drove a Lotus! But his father was desperately hoping that Glen would be admiring *him*, emulating *him*, rôle modeling on *him*. That is a father's understandable and natural desire, and our Father in heaven is no different. We are created in his image, and our desires, such as wanting our children to admire and imitate us, are quite often a reflection of his.

In fact, he tells us that many times in the Bible, and it is the overall message of the Sermon on the Mount in Matthew chapters 5, 6 and 7, summarized in the verse, 'Be perfect, just as your Father in heaven is perfect.' (Matthew 5:48). "Be like me," He says.

I want to please God? Then I shall try and be like him. I shall imitate him, speak like he speaks, say the things he says, and do the things that he does. If I can be a small version of God in my community and church, he will be so pleased. It's all to do with relationship, and I want to please him. This will not guarantee answered prayer – but it is all part of the overall equation!

## Faith to Launch Out

I was friendly with a great man of God called Harry Greenwood. If ever I knew a man of faith, Harry was that man. If he believed he had heard from God, he hung in there, like Abraham aged one hundred years believing he would have a son. And sometimes he would just go for it, like Peter believing the crippled man at the Gate Beautiful would leap to his feet. On one occasion, Harry really believed the Lord wanted him to have a particular car, a Citroën-Maserati. But he 'lived by faith', receiving no salary and having no contract of employment – he simply believed that as long as the Lord wanted him 'in ministry', he would provide for him. Harry had driven various cars at different times, but now he really believed the Lord wanted him to have a Citroën-Maserati. I did not know much about cars, and absolutely nothing about Citroën-Maseratis. Nevertheless, it was just a few months later, when I had hired a 600-seater hall in Norwich and distributed leaflets to let the city know that 'a healing evangelist' would be preaching and healing the sick, that a Citroën-Maserati (one of only seventeen in the country) drew up outside my home. Okay, he reversed it into my gate-post and his face fell a mile – but Harry, man of faith, had received his Citroën-Maserati.

Faith! Harry had faith – but he told me about someone who he felt had more. He was in the USA, where he was preaching and healing the sick in the way that evangelists do. After he had spoken one evening, a line of people formed, waiting for him to lay his hands upon them and ask the Lord to heal them. A little girl arrived at the front of the queue, and Harry asked her what she wanted from Jesus.

"I have a big hole in this tooth, and I would like Jesus to make it better," she replied. Harry stared into her mouth, where there was an obvious cavity in one of her teeth.

At that time he just could not realistically believe that the Lord would heal the tooth. So he laid his hands on the little girl, prayed to the Lord to heal her, and then physically pushed her along so that the next person in the queue was now in front of him. He told me that he did not really want to see the tooth, as he was not 'in great faith' to see a healed molar in her mouth! Harry laid his hand on the next person and started asking the Lord for healing, when there were a number of gasps and utterances of 'Praise God' from an area to his right. Quickly concluding his prayer for the person in front of him, he turned to see a small crowd of people gazing into the mouth of the girl with the hole in the tooth.

"It's healed," said one.

"It's gold," said another.

"Praise God", said several more.

"Let me have a look," said Harry, and gazing into the girl's mouth, could hardly believe what he saw. The tooth had been filled with gold!

"It's been filled!" said Harry. "Your tooth is Okay again."

The response of the little girl probably remains with all who heard it.

"But that's what I asked Jesus for," she said, with an air of innocence and naivety. And that is what she got!

\* \* \*

Harry-type faith is OK. Little girl-type faith is OK. But we do need faith. Well, most do, though I have my doubts about

Frank, who I wrote about in an earlier chapter, and who shouted to God when the truck ran back into him!

Hebrews 11:6 says that 'without faith, it is impossible to please God'. So we need faith in order to please God. What is faith exactly? Unbelievers sometimes think it is a form of 'hoping', but the faith that God teaches us about in the Bible is different from that. There is strong assurance, such that the apostles and others in the New Testament church would *expect* healing and miracles to take place. Peter simply told the crippled man at the temple gate to 'get up'. That was more than a hope!

Hebrews 11:1 tells us that 'faith is the substance of things hoped for, and the evidence of things not seen'. That is strong stuff – *substance, evidence*. It speaks of assurance, such as Peter and others demonstrated so often. But where does such faith come from? We read in Romans 10:17 that it comes from hearing God. Not from trying hard, or even reading the Bible, but by *hearing God*. Which, of course, brings us back to relationship. We need to *hear*. When reading the Bible, or listening to someone preach, or walking down the road, or sitting by the fire.... we need to have ears open to God, because once you hear *God* tell you something, you have unshakeable faith. You *know*, because the Lord has told you. That is why Peter and others could confidently pray for, and at times command, healing.

We learn in all things, if we are wise. Maybe we will make mistakes, but if we are never willing to make a mistake, we will never launch out at all, and our lives will be rather dull. Have ears to hear, and respond. Use this gift of God, and it will grow. It's not simply for healing cripples and raising the dead, but for ordinary people like you and me in our ordinary everyday lives.

We had been married a few months, and decided to buy our first house. It was under construction, and the builder told us that we could move in on 12th December 1969. Some time later, there were problems relating to the building work, and we were then informed that the completion of the property would be significantly delayed. My wife, however, heard from God that the house would in fact be finished by the original date, so we made the necessary arrangements with a furniture removal company, and gave notice to the owners of the rented accommodation where we were living. Guess when the house was finished? 12th December 1969, and we moved straight in. Having heard God on that, we felt able to step out in faith over other matters later.

Relationship is at the heart of pleasing God, and it is in having a real relationship with him that we hear him. It may be the still, small voice, or the scripture that has such life that it virtually leaps out of the page at us, or it might be that inner witness of the Spirit whispering, "That's Me" when somebody shares a vision, or a dream, or is simply in conversation with us. Jesus said that the words that he spoke were 'spirit and life' (John 6:63) – and they still are. Learn to recognise it, and *in faith*, launch out. It pleases him. Once again, launching out does not guarantee answered prayer, but it is an important part of the overall equation that makes up our relationship with him.

Remember the remark attributed to the golfer Gary Player. His ball was on the edge of a large green, and the hole was towards the opposite side, around sixty feet away. He was not expected to sink it, but the crowd held their breath as he fixed his eye, first on the hole and then on the ball, before tapping it across the green. It rolled and rolled and appeared to be on target, until – wow, it *was* on target and dropped into the hole with a satisfying 'plop'. His caddy looked at him and said something I would not have thought he was permitted to say. His words were, "That was lucky, Mr. Player." Gary Player's response was memorable, and can be applied to so many aspects of life, from investing in the Stock Market to pulling out teeth to hearing God speak. He said, "It was indeed lucky, but I have found that the more I practice, the luckier I get!" Listen for God. You have ears to hear – use them. And when you hear, launch out. And the more you practice...

Besides, quite simply, it pleases God.

## Time with the Father

Relationship is covered elsewhere, especially in Chapter 23, but... One big factor in relationship is time spent together. Not because you have to, but because you love to. Not because other things are unimportant, but because the loved person is *more* important. It's true in marriage, and in family – and with our Father. Not to tick a box, not because I have written it here, and not to produce results when you pray, but – because it's a real genuine love relationship.

Some people tell me that prayer is 'difficult'. I guess some people would say that time with their wife or husband is 'difficult'! It is about relationship, and it is about love. Why do I like to spend time with Wendy? Because I love her. Why do I love her? Well, it's the person she is, plus the fact that she loves *me*. I look at what she does and listen to what she says, and I love her. She is so kind to people (especially me), and so sensitive to people's needs (especially mine), and so generous with her time, money, catering skills, gift of hosting, etc. etc. etc. – I love Wendy! I want to spend time with this wonderful, extraordinary person.

It's pretty much the same with my Heavenly Father. I look at what he does – the beauty of creation, the provision for every creature, the way he has reached out to people throughout history, the things he says, the promises he makes, the love he shows to his children, the sacrificial love of sending Jesus who revealed even more of the Father to us. Suffering for us, dying for us, changing our lives, bringing fulfilment, giving us purpose.... All these things, and more, reveal something of the Person of the Father. He is wonderful, and I love him. So I enjoy being with him, often sensing his presence, and hearing him speak quietly to my spirit. These times are precious, special, and important to him and to me. And like any father enjoying the fact that his child enjoys spending time with him, God is pleased.

This again does not guarantee that any particular prayer will be answered, but it is part of that overall equation again. It is one more vital component of a life lived enjoying relationship with God himself.

## Holiness

"Do you teach holiness?" asked a lady over the Internet. She was speaking about *Liberty!* – the church that meets in our home.

"No – we tell people to indulge in the sins of the flesh, and wallow in depraved carnality," I was tempted to answer.

\* \* \*

There is no getting away from the fact that the Lord expects holiness from his people. "Be holy, as I am holy," is a repeated exhortation in the Old Testament, and especially in the book of Leviticus. Jesus promised the gift of the Holy Spirit to those who followed him, and in numerous places, we are urged to live lives worthy of him. Do we not realise that we (plural) are a 'temple' of the Holy Spirit (1 Corinthians 3:16), and indeed individually this is true too (1 Corinthians 6:19). So keep the temple holy, we are taught, with clean living, such as is expected of children of God.

There has been a tendency for churches to teach holiness in a legalistic manner in the past, such that people try and keep rules. But their hearts may not be right, and pride can easily creep in. We are called to live by *grace,* knowing that all our sin – past, present and future – is covered by the blood of Jesus, and where there is a real revelation of this, a person's life will exude holiness as a big Thank-you to the Lord for what he has done. Where there is unclean living and persistent, recurring sin, any profession of 'living by grace' emanates from head knowledge and *not* from heart revelation.

David committed adultery and (as good as) murder. But he was also a man after God's own heart. Samson followed the craving of his flesh, but the Lord anointed him as a judge over Israel. Nobody except Jesus is perfect, but we do have a striking contrast of holiness and unholiness in the lives of each of these two men. Their example is in no way an excuse for others to adopt that style, and if David and Samson had not fallen in their respective ways, might not they have known even greater blessing and fruitfulness? But they were forgiven – their sin was removed, 'as far as the east is from the west,' Psalm 103:12.

I find the situation of the church in Corinth to be helpful with regard to holiness. The power and gifts of the Holy Spirit were *so* evident in the church there, and yet there was also immorality, idolatry, division, and many other manifestations of ungodliness and carnality. One might say to Paul, "Come on. You're their apostle. Don't you teach holiness?"

But Paul did teach holiness to this church – a church that knew the power of the Holy Spirit whilst engaging in such carnality. Wendy and I are part of a small church called *Liberty!* We are called to be free – free of legalism, religiosity, and of anything else that might hold us back from serving Jesus. We want to 'give the Church back to Jesus', see him truly being given his place as Head of the Church as well as of this little church, and seeing the Holy Spirit leading in reality. Two things that result from this are, firstly, that we see the gifts of the Holy Spirit in operation, and miracles occurring as prayer is answered. But secondly, the love of God and his obvious power to set people free attracts folk. So people who are damaged (most of us have been), people who are addicted to alcohol, drugs, immorality, and so much more, come along at times. Like Paul, we preach and teach holiness – but people rarely respond instantly. Some do. Some fall back. Some never respond. Many move on. And there are also mature

Christians who join us because the Lord has called them to – and they do not move on.

Do we teach holiness? Yes – and especially in private to those who particularly need to hear it.

We are told to find those things that please the Lord, and holiness is one of them. Clean living from a thankful heart. Psalm 66:18 says that the Lord does not hear us where we 'regard iniquity' in our heart. To say that the blood of Jesus covers all sin such that we can indulge in it without it affecting our walk with God is, to my mind, deception. If we are asking the Lord to hear us and answer us when we call to him, let us live as is fitting for children of a holy God. Clean living. Holiness – it's all part of that relationship.

## Generosity

"Have a drink on me," said the drunken birthday boy. Okay, he was not really a boy, but he was celebrating, and the more his veins were filled with alcohol, the more generous he became. I have been there, in the years before I met the Lord. I was a student with very little money, and occasionally after a night out, I would realise that the alcohol had made me far too generous to others. And likewise, there were also times when others were far too generous to me.

'Be filled with the Spirit,' we read in Ephesians 5:18. When Jesus comes into a person's life, they change. They become more like Christ. Their values, speech, and general conduct become godly. When we are truly filled with the Spirit, we become generous. Ridiculously generous. Scrooge is liberated! We are like drunks – giving, giving, giving. And if we are not, yet consider ourselves godly, we are deceived. The kingdom of God is no place for meanies, and those who are close to the Lord grow like him.

Jesus said, "Give, and it shall be given unto you." Luke 6:38. Miracles, healings, answered prayers… Our God is not a slot machine, where you can give so much to your church, to missionaries, to charity, etc. in order to receive something back from him, but – he loves his people to be generous.

Are you a meanie? Then start pushing the boat out. Are you on a modest income, and need to budget carefully? Start pushing that boat out – budget a little for giving, not in order 'to get', but because you want to be like God, and because you are a child of His. Yet again, there are no guarantees, except that you will be pleasing him.

## Praise

When we first moved to the city of Norwich, we had a house of modest proportions, though most of the ground floor was our sitting room. There was a small kitchen, a tiny hall and cloakroom, a staircase, and a sitting room. We had welcomed around eight people into that room on Sundays, but after about eighteen months, there were nearer seventy of us. This resulted in overspill into the hall, cloakroom and up the stairs, but most of us were crammed into the sitting room. Teens and twenties sat on the floor, shoulder-to-shoulder and wall-to-wall. It was said that when one stood up, all stood up, because they were stuck to each other! And did we praise our God! It was during one of those evenings that I first sensed the presence of God almost tangibly within the context of praise, as I have done so many times since. We were singing a song of triumphant praise, 'Hallelujah, for the Lord our God the Almighty reigns.' It seemed as though I could have touched him, and there have been many other similar occasions, usually associated with praise. At times, it is as though heaven descends and fills the room where we are meeting, and periodically I tap my toe on the floor to reassure myself that I am still on Planet Earth. Seems silly? But it's that real.

In Psalm 22:3 we are told that the Lord inhabits the praises of his people. You want to see prayers answered, miracles, God at work? Praise him! Why does he come down so close to us at such times? Because he enjoys doing so. He is pleased to be amongst a praising people. Praise him! Please him!

## 'Attitude'

"Well, if he's a politician, he's no good, is he?"

"Have you heard what our church leader is doing *now*? The man's an idiot."

"*How* much is he earning? It's obscene."

Ever heard someone speak like that? Most of us have said similar things at times, and some people deserve such comments. But I am speaking in this section about the person who regularly, predictably, usually, speaks in this way about most people who have authority, or status, or who are successful. The people who so often speak like this, must know that they are like it – but they continue doing it. They criticise their church leaders, their children fall away from the church, and while the parents say they cannot understand why their children do not attend any more, the children have wondered for years why the parents attend at all. Why are they a part of the church when they are always complaining about the leaders? 'If the leaders are such rubbish, why go?' But the 'rubbish' is the value system of the parent, who is quite simply, in rebellion. God hates rebellion. God loves loyalty.

I appreciate that church leaders are not perfect, but in general terms, the Lord has put them there because they are the people he has chosen to lead. Not all, but many. Not all politicians, leaders of British industry, leaders of Trades Unions, professional footballers and other millionaire celebrities are perfect; far from it, but to continually, *regularly*, criticise people with authority, status, success and cash betrays an attitude problem. It is coveting or being jealous of another person's authority, status, success or cash. Stop it. Get delivered.

You want to see answered prayer? You want to see miracles? Then do not rant against the authorities that God has ordained.

'The powers that be are ordained of God.' Rom.13:1. You don't like it? Then get humble, get right before God, and stop bad-mouthing and belly-aching about leaders and those with authority.

What does the Lord require of you? – fairness, kindness and humility (Micah 6:8). Such people are likely to rejoice at answered prayer, and see miracles. Why? Because they are pleasing God.

## Use Your Gift

Wendy's computer was so slow. It took an age to warm up, another age to find a page, sometimes froze or cut out, and was generally so frustrating that she rarely used it. So I splashed out and adorned her study with an Apple iMac. I expected her to be glued to the screen for days, but it was not so. The signal from the router hardly reached the new computer, and a number of passwords were no longer recognised. She felt like giving up, and left her study looking despondent. The result was that both of us were disappointed; Wendy could not use her new gift, and I felt sad that she could not enjoy using such a wonderful piece of kit. But with a little help from a specialist engineer, all was well, she was using it a lot, and we were both happy.

As I mentioned in the last chapter, our Father in heaven has given us gifts. If we do not use them, we are unfulfilled and he is – can one say that God is 'disappointed'? Whether or not God can be disappointed may be a theological issue, but when we use the gifting he has given us, we are fulfilled, the Church is blessed, and our Father is pleased.

What gifting has he given you? Use it. If you do not know what gifting you have been given (and everyone has been given one or more gifts), then ask yourself what works for you? What brings you fulfilment? What gifting do others see in you? – ask them.

Speak to your church leaders about opportunities to move in your calling, and if they say there are none, seek the Lord about changing to another church. You must use your gifting to be fulfilled, to be effective, to build up the church – and to please your Father in heaven.

Eventually, it all comes back to relationship. I love Wendy, and gave her the gift of an iMac. She loves me, and therefore she wanted to use it. Now she has started, she enjoys it, and blesses many folk through the way she uses it. So we are both pleased. There is an obvious parallel with gifting from our Heavenly Father. This is another important way in which we develop our relationship with the Lord – a relationship in which we make requests in prayer and he answers.

* * *

I have outlined some of the ways in which we can please the Lord, and if we love him, this is something that will be important to us. I have already said that God is not a slot-machine where you put in 'generosity' or 'holiness' or anything else, and out pops an answered prayer. It is all about relationship, and where we seek to please the Lord by doing those things that please him, we will bring ourselves closer to him. As I have said earlier, those people I have known, who have seemed to me to have a close relationship with the Lord, have also been people who seemed to receive answers to prayer.

* * *

*'Find out what pleases the Lord.'* Ephesians 5:10 (NIV)

# Chapter 27

# *'Unanswered' Prayer?*

"We prayed for healing for Fred – but he only got worse, and then he died. Well, our prayers *have* been answered, because he's alright now. There's no sickness in heaven, is there?"

\* \* \*

Many of us have heard statements like that. They are proffered as an explanation for apparently unanswered prayer, but for many of us, they just do not stand up.

The statement that Fred is now healed because he is in heaven is quite true, as far as I'm concerned. But to suggest that this is an answer to prayer for healing gives me a problem. Why pray at all? If Fred recovers, their prayer is answered. If Fred gets worse and dies, their prayer is answered. So why pray? What were they praying for? If I pray for a sick person, I am almost always praying that they will recover, and not die from the sickness.

So why do we sometimes *not* see the Lord giving us what we pray for?

## Unknowable

God is God! He is eternal, and intelligent far beyond our comprehension. Job understandably says, 'God is exalted and we do not know him', Job 36:26. This is echoed elsewhere in scripture, and yet there are also references to God being knowable. Here we have a paradox, but let us have a look at it.

His eternal vastness is beyond us. Why? Our intelligence is finite, and yet God is infinite and transcendental, which means that he is in a different spiritual realm, and uniquely so. Look at creation! Let me tell you just a few facts about the human body – and I am quoting from a greetings card I designed a few years ago.

*The human body is truly amazing, way beyond our understanding. So many different organs carrying out so many complex functions, carried by a framework of bones and cartilages that self-lubricate with exactly the correct amount of jelly-like substance; a chemical plant that changes food into living tissue that sees, hears, walks, thinks and has consciousness; a brain that is more complex than any computer ever devised or constructed; lungs containing 300,000 million small blood vessels that could stretch over 1500 miles; each kidney contains 1,000,000 individual filters......*

Try and imagine the intelligence of our Creator – or maybe you think that the human body just came together through accidents and chances. Wow – you really have got much greater faith than me, because I cannot believe that!

Once our brain has developed, we probably have 60 years to study God – if we want to. What hope is there of understanding anymore than a fraction of who he is?

But he is knowable, because Jesus reveals him. The disciples and others met him when he walked this earth. Paul and others met him after the ascension. We too can know him today, which is the message of the gospel.

But, to try and explain everything about God is ridiculous, because he is who he is – eternal, immortal and infinitely beyond the grasp of our human minds. The Trinity is a mystery. He tells us quite clearly in the Bible that he is one (Deuteronomy 6:4 and elsewhere), and yet we also find he refers to himself in plurality as 'us' (Genesis 1:26; 11:7 and elsewhere), and we read of the Father being God, the Son being God, and the Holy Spirit being a person who is God. There are those who have determined to understand this, and the result is that they have either formed, or joined, unitarian cults. One could also take the contentious subject of 'Are we chosen or do we choose?' The Bible teaches both, but there are theologians who, with human understanding, feel compelled to fathom the unfathomable, and in opting exclusively for either 'we are chosen' or 'we choose', cease to uphold the integrity of the scriptures that teach the 'opposing' view. These matters are paradoxes that are beyond human understanding – God is One God and yet three distinct Persons, and we are sovereignly chosen by the Lord whilst also being totally free to choose.

So although there are often clear reasons for some prayers not being answered in the way we might anticipate, we cannot expect to have all the answers to all the questions that we or others may present. God is too big for that! Job and his friends probably felt that they had most of the answers to life's questions, but when they had put forward all the reasons they could think of for Job's suffering, the Lord asked, "And where were you when I created everything?"

But at times we are left asking "Why?" This is probably the prayer I have uttered most in my life. "Why?" Why was this prayer not answered, and that one, and the other one? I pray for healing for someone dying (to my mind prematurely) and they die. Why? I pray for reconciliation where a marriage is breaking down and the children are being harmed and the Christian witness is compromised, and... nothing! Why? These are just some examples, and the answer is – we do not know. Why indeed? We cannot fathom God and find the answer to every question.

There *is* an answer to every question, and a perfect answer at that, but we do not necessarily have access to it. There are some matters that we just have to lay down, and if we do not, we shall be frustrated, troubled, and brought even to the brink of compromise, such as those who have opted for a unitarian God, because they could not comprehend the incomprehensible Trinity.

But we can know God. Jesus is God, as countless scriptures, such as the opening verses of John 1 make abundantly and overwhelmingly clear. You need to have a faulty translation of scripture to possibly think that Jesus is not God. He is the very image of the invisible God, as is stated explicitly in Colossians 1:15. A contradiction? No – a paradox. We cannot understand it, but need to accept it for the simple reason that it is true. Both 'sides' – he is visible, and invisible – are in fact true. 'All Scripture is given by inspiration of God, and is profitable...' 2 Timothy 3:16. There may be much about the Lord that is unknowable, but so much has been revealed by him in and through the Scriptures. Not only have we the Scriptures that have been inspired by him, but we also have the Holy Spirit to give us understanding. We cannot have a total revelation of the infinite God within the covers of a finite book (really, a set of books) – but we have revelation on everything that it is necessary to know.

So why are some prayers not answered? We shall never, ever know, but there are many things that we do know. I have very briefly sketched out below a few reasons that I find helpful.

## Timing

The man born blind in John 9 was seen by the disciples as a sinner. Or maybe his parents were, they suggested. But who really sinned and caused this man to be blind? – No-one, said Jesus; this was for the glory of God. Surely the man had prayed at some time, maybe often, that he would be able to see? But his prayers, if so, had been 'unanswered' at that time. I would imagine that his parents had done so too, when his plight became apparent at an early age. And their prayers too would have been 'unanswered'. But in the wisdom of God, *now* was the time for the man to have his sight restored.

There is so much that we are unaware of regarding the big plan in which the Lord is directing all of history to the return of Jesus. I believe that he desires people to be healthy, but sometimes a delay in healing can accomplish things that instant healing would leave undone. Job was not healed instantly – but he was healed and restored at the right time. And I am sure there are countless other cases where the Lord's timing is different than we would wish, or indeed, can understand.

## Persistence

Ask, seek, knock, we are told by Jesus in Matthew 7:7. There are times when we ask, and the Lord immediately moves to grant the request. Instantly. Immediately. Wendy and I prayed for Emilio in Mexico, and instantly his arm straightened. But sometimes we have to seek the will of God, and we find that the answer does not come immediately. My wife and I felt that it was time to move from Shaftesbury, in Dorset, UK, but were unsure where the Lord wanted us to live. We prayed for some months before somebody in a meeting had a vision of a knight on a chessboard, and we realised that we were to move North one unit, and East two units – into East Anglia. But there are also situations where we need to *knock*.

How do we 'knock' in our praying? Jesus told a parable concerning a woman who went to an 'unjust judge' with a request. She was just a widow. She had no clout. The judge did not care about people, and did not fear God. What hope was there for her? You can read the story in Luke 18:1-8. Her hope was in persistence, because she tired the judge out, and he was so fed up with her persistent petitioning that he granted her request. The lesson? – we have a far greater standing than that widow did in New Testament times, and our Heavenly Father cares for us far more than the unjust judge did for the widow.

So persist. Why? Patience and persistence are character building. Will we persist in what we believe to be the will of God? If we do, we may well be rewarded.

Are we truly serious about laying hold of God in prayer? Jacob wrestled with God, and would not let go until God had blessed him. You can read about this in Genesis 32:22-32. I really do not think that the Lord does this to see how serious we are with him – he knows that already. But we do not know this, and it reveals our heart to ourselves, and if we are deficient in being serious, we can do something about it once we know this.

Do you remember the time when Jesus prayed for a blind man, who then said he could see, but not clearly? He could see men as 'trees walking'. You can read this story in Mark 8. So Jesus prayed for him again – and he was completely healed. Be encouraged that Jesus did not have 100% success in this case the first time he prayed! Persist. Keep praying, if necessary.

## Lack of faith.

In Matthew 13, towards the end of the chapter, we read that Jesus went to His home town and could do few miracles, because of their lack of faith. *Jesus* could do few miracles? So the faith, or lack of it, in those around us can affect 'answers to prayer'. Don't blame others, because that may not be the reason – but be aware that the faith, or lack of it in those around us, can have a significant effect. So, don't blame yourself either!

## Discipline

There are those who say that the Lord *never, ever* really disciplines His children. But the people of Israel were his kids, and he disciplined them. Miriam was smitten with leprosy because of her rebellious attitude towards the Lord's leaders, but it was for a short period of time. Read about it in

Numbers 12. She learnt something concerning who is Boss, and of how she should relate to his chosen leaders.

I have a lot of time for those who are referred to at the present time as 'grace teachers'. Some may teach in a manner that leans towards antinomianism (a heresy that teaches that it is OK to sin, because Jesus has paid the price already), but others are faithful to scripture and are correcting legalistic tendencies in many other Christian leaders. However, reading a book on grace recently, I have noticed that more than once the writer poses the question, "Would any father inflict sickness or disease on his child in order to discipline them?" The obvious answer is "No", but that begs the question, 'why was Miriam afflicted with a bout of leprosy?' She was one of God's people, and yet the Lord disciplined her in this way, which also served as a warning to others who might be tempted to rebel against God's appointed leadership.

I would not want to point the finger and cause anyone to come under condemnation about sickness or any other problem that was not resolved through prayer. However, there is a Biblical case for seeing sickness and other difficulties as, at times, the discipline of the Father.

## Mystery!

And so we come back to the mystery of God. He is Eternal and Infinite. In Deuteronomy 29:29, we are told that there are some things that God reveals to us, and some things that he does not. They are 'secret' things, and will remain so. Do not spend too much time trying to understand those things that are not understandable at this time. Just accept that God is so much greater than us.

Jehovah's Witnesses, Mormons, Unitarians and others, have tried to understand *everything* about the Lord and his ways – and have ended up as a cult. Don't! There are mysteries in the kingdom, but the Lord has shown us everything we need to know.

Pray. Have faith. Develop your relationship with the Lord. If he's done it for Wendy and me, he can do it for you. Signs? Wonders? Miracles? Our God specialises in these things. We see through a glass darkly, but will one day see clearly. Let us move forward in the abundant light we have, and not get too hung up on what we do not presently understand.

\* \* \*

May you have the grace to step out in prayer, and having developed your relationship with the living God, may you pray in the Name of Jesus. May you see the sick healed, the oppressed delivered, the needy provided for and the captives released, bringing pleasure to the Father and honour to the Son, as you move out with Jesus to bring him glory and extend his kingdom here on earth.

\* \* \*

*'And whatever you ask in My name, that I will do, that the Father may be glorified in the Son. If you ask anything in My name, I will do it.' John 14:13,14*

*'The secret things belong to the LORD our God, but those things which are revealed belong to us and our children forever, that we may do all the words of this law.'*
*Deuteronomy 29:29*

# Appendix

## And Finally, the Word of God Says...

*Is anything too hard for the LORD?* Genesis 18:14

*I call out to the LORD, and he answers me from his holy mountain.* Psalm 3:4

*The Lord will hear when I call to Him.* Psalm 4:3

*I sought the Lord, and He heard me, and delivered me from all my fears.* Psalm 34:4

*Enter into His gates with thanksgiving, and into His courts with praise.* Psalm 100:4

*The LORD is near to all who call on him, to all who call upon him in truth.* Psalm 145:18

*The LORD is far from the wicked: but he hears the prayer of the righteous.* Proverbs 15:29

*Ask, and it will be given to you; seek, and you will find; knock, and it will be opened to you.* Matthew 7:7

*For with God nothing will be impossible.* Luke 1:37

*I give you authority... over all the power of the enemy...* Luke 10:19

*Our Father in heaven...* Luke 11:2

*Whatever you ask in My name, that will I do, that the Father may be glorified in the Son. If you ask anything in My name, I will do it.* John 14:13,14

*Now, Lord, look on their threats, and grant to Your servants that with all boldness they may speak Your word, by stretching out Your hand to heal, and that signs and wonders may be done through the name of Your holy Servant Jesus.*

*And when they had prayed, the place where they were assembled together was shaken; and they were all filled with the Holy Spirit, and they spoke the word of God with boldness.* Acts 4:29-31

*I will pray with the spirit, but I will also pray with the understanding. I will sing praise with the spirit, and I will also sing with the understanding.* 1 Corinthians 14:15

*Now to Him who is able to do exceeding abundantly above all that we ask or think, according to the power that works in us.* Ephesians 3:20

*Be anxious for nothing; but in every thing by prayer and supplication with thanksgiving let your requests be made known to God.* Philippians 4:6

*Pray without ceasing. 1 Thessalonians 5:17*

*I will therefore that men pray everywhere, lifting up holy hands, without wrath and doubting.* 1 Timothy 2:8

*Confess your faults one to another, and pray one for another, that you may be healed. The effectual fervent prayer of a righteous man avails much.* James 5:16

*He cares for you.* 1 Peter 5:7

# Team Barrie

Given the opportunity, I would love to stand on a platform and read out a list of those people who have helped me write this book, to rapturous applause from the assembled readers. As a youngster, enthralled by Noddy, Big Ears, the Famous Five, the Secret Seven, Long John Silver, and a host of other characters who walked across the pages of my childhood reading, I never gave a thought to the process by which those books had come into my possession. But in later years, I realised that at some point, somebody had sat down, presumably at a typewriter, and produced a manuscript. And that after much thought. It was years later that I started reading the *Acknowledgements*, either at the front or back of a tome, because someone had said that if my name was written there, I would want people to read it. It was the same with the credits at the beginning or end of a movie. I can understand why some people skip these items, but they did open up to me the realisation of the multitude involved in the process by which a book makes its lengthy journey from the mind of the author, through the hands of family and friends, proof-readers, publishing staff, and typesetters, to those working in bookshops or online booksellers.

At a personal level, I feel tremendously indebted to so many people who have helped me, and assisted in the production of this book, along the way. I will mention the more significant ones, and ask those omitted to forgive that oversight.

Jesus is at the centre of my universe. He changed my life forever back in October 1965, though some would say it was almost two thousand years earlier. He moved me from darkness to light, from death to life, from hell to heaven – and gave me Life with a capital 'L', which transformed me from an unfulfilled atheist to a fulfilled, born-again child of God. The Holy Spirit eternally seeks to glorify Jesus, and we are urged to be co-workers with him in that work, which pleases the Father. One God, three Persons. I do not understand that, and nor am I meant to, but I accept it and rejoice in it. No-one has been more important to me in the production of this book than the Holy Spirit, whose help I have sought daily. No one is more important than Jesus, to whom this book, by the grace of God, points. And there is no-one I want to please more than the Father, who has been the very best *Abba*, or Dad, to me since before I ever knew him.

On earth, the evangelist Don Double has been my spiritual father for many years. When I have entered difficult times, he has always been one of the first on the telephone, and he and his late, greatly missed, wife Heather, were always there for me. Don continues to be a strength, encouragement and inspiration to so many people. Although busily engaged in evangelistic ministry, he has very generously given hours of his time sifting through this book and advising and encouraging me in so many ways. I will always be indebted to Don.

Many of the incidents related in this book occurred within the context of the church called *Liberty!* which currently meets in our home, and occasionally in halls. A number of people from the church were a tremendous support and encouragement during our early days, and some have continued to be. I want to mention some by name – Barry Harvey, Colin and Merry Huxtable, John Alam, Karina Sayer, Shirlene Phillips, Malcolm and Moira Springall, James and Amanda Cullabine, Freya Hayton, and most of all, my wife Wendy. Other incidents have involved Norwich Full Gospel Businessmen's Fellowship, which often holds meetings in our home. A number of members and their wives have been amazingly supportive and encouraging during the past few years that I have been president – Mike and Lois Wiltshire, John and Sue Wright, Malcolm and Moira Springall, Gordon and Jackie Bambridge, Rod Robertson and his late wife Chrissie, Robert and Margaret Osborne, Kevin and Coleen Gotts, and the late Tony Gardiner and his wife Jean. Mark Skittrall, Ivor Boulton and Neil Claxton also deserve a mention.

Barry Harvey has again been my main proof-reader, and I am indebted to him for hours and hours of meticulously sifting through the spelling, grammar, factual aspects, matters of doctrine, and so much more. As a first-former at The Paston School in 1956, little did I guess that Barry Harvey, one of the 'big boys' in the year above me, would one day be my brother in Christ, and help me produce books. Gill Hunkin, secretary to Don Double at Good News Crusade, has also spent several hours reading the manuscript, and generally advising me on content.

The cover design is again the work of Derek Blois, who also played a significant part in deciding the title (and not for the first time). Derek has become something of a celebrity artist in recent years, and deservedly so. His work can be viewed at the PictureCraft Gallery & Exhibition Centre, in Holt, Norfolk, and online at www.picturecraftgallery.co.uk/derek-blois-bahons-aiea/

My four daughters continually encourage and delight me. They still laugh at my jokes, and have always 'been there for me'. They were excited when my first book was published some years ago now, and continue to enthuse over my writing today. I have been blessed with such a wonderful family. Thank you Sarah, Rachel, Naomi and Deborah.

When the Lord brought Wendy into my life, I had no idea of just how greatly he was blessing me, or with such a priceless gift. We still keep pinching ourselves to make sure we are not dreaming. It was in our early days that I looked across the table of the restaurant in which we were seated, and thought, "You are so beautiful." When gardening, Wendy looks like a gardener – but she scrubs up well, and there are many occasions when I just have to tell her, "Darling, you are so beautiful." Perhaps I am also seeing those other unseen aspects of beauty with which Wendy adorns my life. She is the most generous, sensitive, welcoming, kindest person I have met. To everyone. And especially, to me. She is so patient as I sit tapping away at my iPad, or vanish for a few hours into my study in order to edit, print, market, email, and attend to so many other necessary 'book' chores. Romance, restaurants, hosting church in our home, entertaining multitudes around our dining table, feeding little short of 5,000 on numerous occasions – my lover, my best friend, my partner in kingdom business and sister in the family of God – I love you so much, and thank the Lord daily for bringing you into my life.

And finally I thank you, the reader. Thank you for reading thus far – well done! And for those who write to me, and email me, with kind words, and who recommend my books to their friends, I am sincerely grateful. May you know richly the blessing of the living God – who answers the prayers of his children when they cry out to him.

# THERE MUST BE MORE
# TO LIFE THAN THIS!

## How to know the God of the Bible in Everyday Life

by Barrie Lawrence

Published by New Wine Press (2012)

Barrie writes in his own distinctive style of incidents in his life that can only be described as amazing coincidences – or acts of God!

Barrie sent a paperback book to a patient, as he thought it would be helpful. The patient's wife took it from the postman, panicked, and called the emergency services to say a bomb had just been delivered. Why? A lady Barrie had known several years earlier, was woken up in the night to hear the Lord say to her, "Pray for Barrie Lawrence." Years later she was amazed to find out just why! And there was the time when a teapot prevented Barrie from really enjoying life as it was meant to be. How could that be? And then again there was the time when he and his wife were called to a school to heal a boy with a deformed arm – and the whole class were waiting to watch the miracle.

Not without humour, Barrie writes of the ways *he* has been challenged on various occasions in his life, of his successes and his failures. It's OK to laugh at him at times, because he does so himself, but you may also want to weep with him as he opens his heart about coping with difficulties and heartbreaks. Above all, it is an inspiring book that seeks to lift the reader onto a higher plane in life.

The first half of the book, part one, comprises fifteen short chapters of true stories from Barrie's own life, while part two has a clear message – "If He's done it for me, He can do it for you!" In fact, part two is a reader-friendly guide to help anyone to come to know the God who we read about in the Bible.

If there are times when you think to yourself, "There must be more to life than this," then this book is a *must-read* for you!

*Available from www.amazon.co.uk and all good bookshops.*

A brilliant book by Barrie Lawrence. For anyone asking, **'Is there more to life than this?'** the author reveals a resounding 'Yes'. He shares his own journey of faith with refreshing candour – and then shows how the reader can experience Life with a capital L.

> **Michael Wiltshire**, *author and journalist, and a director of FGB, the world's largest fellowship for Christian businessmen.*

Barrie Lawrence writes for Christians who compare their uneventful lives to all the excitement they read about in the Bible, and want to experience more of the latter. He shares some of his life story from nearly 50 years of being a Christian before pointing his readers to pointers for experiencing God for themselves. A sincere and candid little book.

> **Christianity Magazine**, *April 2013*

Barrie has an infectious enthusiasm about the things of God and a burning desire to share them with others. The underlying theme is the breaking in of the supernatural to ordinary lives, and the importance of experiencing as well as believing.

> **Network Norwich**, *February 2013*

# CURIOUS PEOPLE, HUMOROUS HAPPENINGS, CROWNS OF GLORY

# A DENTIST'S STORY

by Barrie Lawrence

Published by Grosvenor House Publishing (2014)

After-dinner speaker Barrie Lawrence has been making people laugh – *really* laugh – for years. Now it's your turn to hear his unbelievably funny, sometimes poignant stories from dental school, surgery and life. How did a pet frog lead to a successful career of seven dental surgeries and a bookshop? And of course, he was a student during those years known as the 'Swinging Sixties!'

How can a filling take five hours to complete, and why did one of the lecturers at his dental school describe Barrie qualifying as 'like letting a monkey loose with a pistol'?

Read of some of those incidents and memories that have been making people smile for years when Barrie has been engaged in after-dinner speaking – or simply to the local Women's Institute. Do families of five really share just one toothbrush between them? Do that many dentures sail away down the toilet every winter? Have you ever come across people who share a set of false teeth between them?

But something happened while Barrie was training at the London Hospital – something that was even more important than training as a dentist!

You'll laugh, you'll cry, and most important of all, you will be inspired.

*Available from www.amazon.co.uk in the United Kingdom, and www.amazon.com in North America, and from all good bookshops*

* * *

"A refreshing delight. The author succeeds in maintaining interest by careful selection of anecdotes combined with a light-hearted tone and appropriate pace. I would recommend this book to anybody... looking for something uncomplicated and entertaining."

British Dental Journal, Review by T. Doshi,<br>December 2014

"An entertaining and encouraging read." **Network Norwich.**

# PATIENTS FROM HEAVEN –
## and Other Places!

By Barrie Lawrence

Published by Grosvenor House (2015)

Baron Goldfinger seemed to have stepped straight off the James Bond movie set, Tad the Pole caused the nurses to swoon, while Misty, the flirtatious American lady, suddenly vanished – probably murdered, said the police. These and dozens of other colourful characters walk across the pages of *Patients From Heaven – and Other Places!* During nearly forty years of practice in dental surgery, a wealth of fascinating personalities passed through his surgery. Some were from heaven – and some were from other places! Laugh, smile, gasp, cry, and simply be inspired as you read through these engaging stories from real life.

Available from www.amazon.co.uk (UK), www.amazon.com (North America) and all good bookshops.

\* \* \*

"Barrie introduces us to some of the most memorable people he met in this lovely and engaging memoir, the follow-up of his well-received *A Dentist's Story*. This is a lively read – he has a real way with a tale that keeps you turning the pages. Barrie is a practising Christian, but he doesn't hit you over the head with it; only mentioning it 'as and when' to put his story into context. An enjoyable – and rather uplifting – read."

*Eastern Daily Press, Review by Trevor Heaton, June 2015*

The style of writing reflects Barrie's skill as an engaging and very humorous after dinner speaker. He starts with those (patients) that became friends, or had something that endeared them to him and his staff; others made them laugh, or simply left them feeling better.

How does he depict patients from the *Other Place?* His belief as a born-again Christian, he says, changed everything including the way he sees other people. Courteously, he also sees this category of people with emotions, maybe struggling with relationships or finance. Chapters like "Blue Murder, a Pink Ear, Bubbles and a Bad Smell", "Nice and Nasty" and "The Gift of the Gab" have to be read.

Barrie balances his stories with patient's perceptions about him, with one patient calling him "a dangerous man".

His previous title *A Dentist's Story* concluded with an appendix of dental jokes and this time there is an appendix of anecdotes concerning encounters with members of the police force. Chapters including "The Man in Black", "Idiot!", "The Insurance Fraud?" and "A Carnivorous Villain" leave the reader entertained and bursting with laughter.

This book can easily be read and savoured like a meal with many courses over a period, or devoured in one long sitting. Ideal as a holiday read and to pass on.

*Network Norwich, Review by*
*Kevin Gotts, August 2015*